J'AIME NEW YORK

150 culinary destinations for food lovers.

[signature: Ducasse]

—

CO-AUTHOR
ALEX VALLIS

PHOTOGRAPHY
PIERRE MONETTA

ART DIRECTION
PIERRE TACHON

—

ALAIN DUCASSE
PUBLISHING

« For my wife, Gwénaëlle, with whom I have shared
many New York discoveries in the city where we met.
To Arzhel and Daé, whose curiosity will without
a doubt be nurtured in exploring the Big Apple
together. »

Alain Ducasse

This is not a cookbook, but a food diary. It is a visual narrative of the energy and culture that defines New York. It's a city that blends, mends, and tests, and on the *Big Night* of my first restaurant in the United States, I realized I had a lot to learn about the Big Apple!

My first trip to New York, as a young chef, was in 1976. All these years . . . I can't say enough about this city — the diversity of people, contrast between modernity and history, and its countless alternatives. New York's resilient spirit continues to inspire me.

I have wandered the five boroughs in search of outstanding culinary adventures — a Proustian thrill at a Brooklyn soda fountain, the taste of extraordinary craftsmanship in a fried potato and menu of dipping sauces, an appetite for over-the-top barbecue. Encounters with an endearing waiter who began the conversation by writing down my menu on the paper tablecloth, a hot dog purist, perched at an espresso bar inevitably getting the "locals only" insight into the city...

All of these New York moments, their sights and sounds, their emotions provide so much optimism, continuing to feed the city's cultural imagination and regeneration. I have never felt so alive with a sense of discovery as I do here, never too sure of knowing what something tastes like. This is a city that teaches me about food, about people, about myself. And I experience the city each time I return like it's the first time.

Fast-forward 30 years, the test of time and the result is my New York on a plate. But it's only a snapshot. Other places are already opening, in the works, and that's why I keep coming back.

JE T'AIME, NEW YORK!

DAN BARBER

——

Chef Alain Ducasse pulled his red, open-topped jeep into a clearly illegal space in front of the long, sweeping staircase of the Hotel de Paris, just steps from the famous Monte Carlo casino where his restaurant, Louis XV, resides. Resplendent in his crisp chef's whites and dark sunglasses, he hopped from the jeep and took the stairs two at a time.

I was twenty-four, dressed in my lone button-down jacket and tie, standing frozen near the bottom of the same stairs. It was late in the afternoon as the Riviera sun glazed the central square of Monte Carlo. I swear I remember the details this way, like a scene from a movie that never leaves your head, not only because I had just emerged from what I knew to have been the defining meal of my life, but because to a young, hapless line cook from America, Ducasse looked very much like a movie star. And in many ways he was.

This was the early 1990s, before the razzmatazz of the Food Channel and the chef's confessional, before Facebook, Twitter, and YouTube. In those days, all the great chefs (not only the very few like Ducasse, who had just earned his coveted third Michelin star) were inaccessible: because of this, they appeared like distant constellations — dazzling, mysterious, unknowable. They were judged not by what they said or thought, but by what they cooked. Their cuisine spoke for who they were, and it said it all.

Normally I would have stood and gawked. Lowly cooks like me did not talk directly to chefs, unless invited (and we were never invited). But something came over me, instinct helped along by a healthy dose of lunchtime wine, and I ran back up the stairs after the chef before he could escape.

For the past year I had struggled as a lowly line cook in Paris, seeing little of the city and nothing of France. Part of what had kept me going through the drudgery was the knowledge that when my employment was over, I was making a pilgrimage south, to Le Louis XV, to experience what the French, and soon the world, was talking about. I saved one thousand French francs — enough for the TGV, a youth hostel, and this one meal.

I dined alone at a corner table, and I still remember the taste of the pea soup. It was an ode to a special pea of the region, which were impossibly sweet, triple peeled, and puréed. I had never tasted anything like it and doubt I ever will again. The bread cart, with fifteen different breads to choose from, each as distinctive and delicious as the last, including a borage bread — a soft green doughy roll with a gentle cucumber-like aroma. The fraises des bois, with mascarpone cheese sorbet and warm strawberry sauce, was a revelation because it was a dessert of such simplicity and sincerity I very nearly wept, tasting that first bite. Ducasse has cautiously described his cooking as "rustic Mediterranean — for me the best cooking is 'women's cuisine,' the old home cooking — that's where everything good always comes from." And that's what it tasted it like — home.

I know what you're thinking. The meal was so delicious because of the context. After struggling for a year in the confines of a tyrannical French kitchen, how could dining in a room of such lavishness and grandeur, a place that appeared to have been transported straight from the Palace of Versailles itself, be anything other than extraordinary? That may be true. But the larger truth is that the meal was at once luxurious — gold, gilt, busts, and flower arrangements as tall as trees and also deeply humble — peas, bread, fruit, and cheese. The juxtaposition proved the point — that to experience great cuisine, to soak in a sense of history and place, the pomp and circumstance are not necessary.

I got to Ducasse at the top of the stairs, cutting him off just before he entered his restaurant. At first he stepped back, my abruptness interrupting the scene like a car crash. But after a moment, he looked calm, almost to the point of diffidence. "Chef Ducasse," I said, extending my hand and introducing myself. "I've just had the best meal of my life."

head whirling, and then I rushed off to change my TGV reservation, pay for another night at the youth hostel, and get myself to the casino. (Where, I'm afraid, my luck changed. I lost 150 francs at blackjack within the first fifteen minutes.)

At lunch the next day, the waiter asked if I'd like to see the menu. I said I'd have whatever the chef wanted to send me. He looked mildly confused, but nodded politely and disappeared. The second extraordinary meal of my life followed — including a course of pasta with tomato and basil, and a stew of garden vegetables with Ligurian olive oil, both so evocative of the Riviera, I felt drunk from the feeling of connection alone. It was like eating southern France on a plate.

And then, four hours later, a bill. It was for 400 francs and I nearly fainted. "But monsieur," I said to the waiter in my best French, "Chef Ducasse invited me."

"Chef Ducasse?" he said, slowly repeating my words and raising an eyebrow. "Invited. You." Having waited a year, perhaps my entire young adult life to finally be treated as someone important, I now felt like a fraud. He disappeared, and a manager returned. I explained to him about the exchange on the stairs, the impromptu invitation, my change of plans. He gave me a similarly skeptical — if slightly kinder — look, and presented me a few minutes later with a new bill, 50 percent off the original.

I still didn't have that much cash, but I handed over my father's American Express card, which he had given me for emergen-

"Oh yes? Where?" he asked, winking. And then he said: "You're headed over to the casino, no?" When I told him I had come to Monte Carlo only for the meal and was heading back in the morning, he said, simply: "Go to the casino. Change your plans. Come back to my restaurant for lunch." I was twenty-four, and Alain Ducasse wanted me to return as his guest.

"Bien Sur, chef," I said, half-bowing. He shook my hand and wished me luck at the blackjack table. I stood there a moment,

cies only. A passionate food lover himself, I figured he would understand.

Two decades later, reading this wonderful book about New York, I was transported right back to those two meals in Monte Carlo, reminded (as I have been reminded many times since) of Ducasse's unique ability to capture and convey the true essence of a place.

In the spirit of Alex de Tocqueville, a Frenchmen who famously described America in the 1800s better than any American, Ducasse introduces you to a gastronomic tour of New York that I'm willing to bet most native New Yorkers don't know (I am one of them). He also somehow makes you feel, with each turn of the page, that you are in the very best version of New York, smelling the just-baked baklava from an extraordinary little bakery in Queens, sipping a perfect, bracing espresso at an East Village cafe and hurrying along the avenue to get to the best arepas ever made.

What you are holding is a handsome book, but it's a generous one, too. In its mix of simplicity and imagination, it manages to be simultaneously sensational

and comforting, which isn't a half-bad description of the genius of Ducasse's cooking. Reading through this book, you feel like you've been there, to the real New York. And by the end of it, in fact you have.

CON TEN TS

New York, NY   019

Urban pastoral   169

Capital of the world   353

Sweet life   525

NEW
YORK
NY

21 West 52nd ST
NY, NY 10019

↑ '21' Club

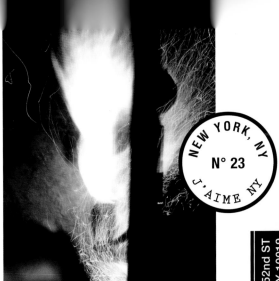

'21' CLUB

A former speakeasy during Prohibition, '21' evolved into a meeting place for power-ful New Yorkers, and it offers a window into the city's industrial history as much as Rockefeller Center or Times Square. The setting remains masculine. Men wear jackets, and you can lunch on burgers and Cobb salads in the Bar Room, where for decades toys have dangled like nursery mobiles and delighted visiting tycoons. Business magnate and aviator Howard Hughes started the tradition in 1931 when he spotted a British Airways model plane hanging from the ceiling and retaliated by having the restaurant install a miniature from his own airline, TWA. Befitting the illicit provenance of this place, the most interesting activities still take place underground: the original liquor vault is now a private dining space and wine cellar with collections that belonged to the likes of Gerald Ford and Elizabeth Taylor.

annisa

→ Annisa

ANNISA

The name translates to "women" in Arabic, and there's a feminine intellectual quality to Annisa's Zen setting. After earning a French degree from Columbia University, chef-owner Anita Lo moved to Paris and graduated from the famous cooking school École Ritz-Escoffier. She nods to her Chinese-American upbringing and subsequent travels in dishes like foie gras soup dumplings with ginger and star anise, and sable with crispy tofu in a bonito broth. Wines from female vintners such as Anne-Claude Leflaive of Burgundy and California's Helen Turley pair perfectly with the meal.

13 Barrow ST
NY, NY 10014

→ Annisa

BOARS HEAD COLD CUTS

	LB	BAGEL	HERO		LB	BAGEL	HERO
HAM	8.09	4.19	4.69	GENOA SALAMI	8.29	4.40	4.90
SPICED HAM	5.09	3.05	3.55	PEPPERONI	6.49	3.60	4.10
ROAST BEEF	9.99	4.70	5.20	SICILIAN SALAMI	8.49	4.45	4.95
PASTRAMI	7.89	4.05	4.55	LACEY SWISS	7.29	4.45	4.70
BOLOGNA	4.69	2.95	3.45	AMERICAN CHEESE	5.29	3.35	3.85
LIVERWURST	4.69	2.85	3.45	SWISS CHEESE	6.89	3.90	4.40
TURKEY	8.45	4.25	4.75	PROVOLONE	6.99	3.90	4.70
MAPLE G. HONEY TURKEY	8.79	4.45	4.95	MUNSTER	6.35	3.95	4.25
PEPPER MILL TURKEY	8.79	4.45	5.95	*EXTRAS			
OVEN ROASTED CHICKEN B.	8.79	4.50	5.00				

SALADS

	LB.
TUNA	8.09
CHICKEN	9.19
EGG	6.69
WHITE FISH	10.9

＊EXTRAS

＊ LETTUCE .25
＊ TOMATO .25
＊ ONION .25
＊ CHEESE .60

BAGEL HOLE

Quality old-fashioned bagels have a nice lacquer, since the dough is boiled before baking. Such specimens are still made with malt at this hole-in-the-wall deli, which opened in 1985. Characterized by their compact size, appealingly durable skin, and tender interior, great bagels shouldn't require toasting. That's the opinion here, anyway, where it's verboten. Otherwise, you may very well catch batches warm from the oven and are welcome to enjoy a schmear of cream cheese.

BAGEL HO
of P
BEST BAGELS
718-788-4014

EGG

DAYOLD BAGELS

6 FOR $2.70

400 Seventh AV
Brooklyn, NY 11215

→ Bagel Hole

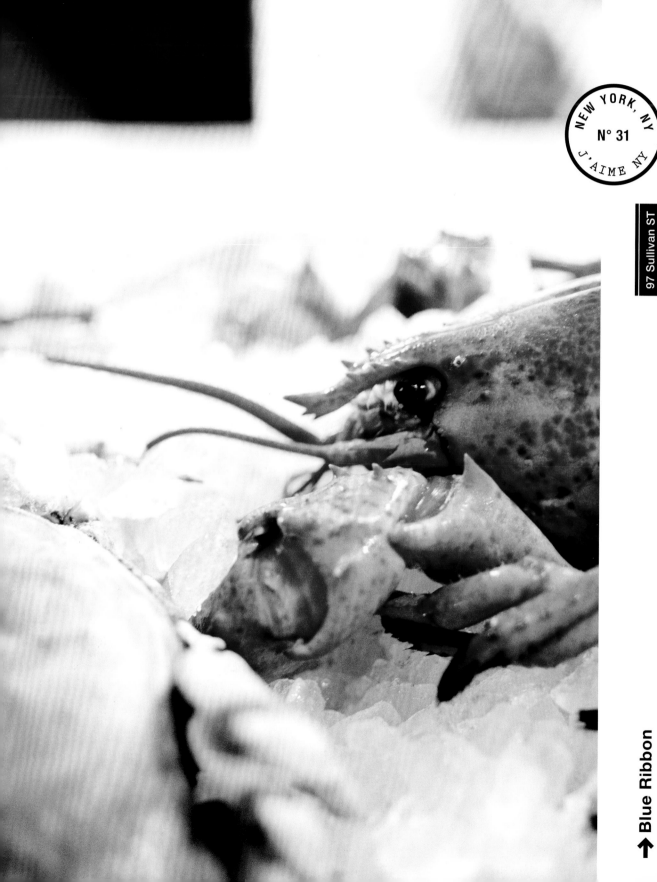

97 Sullivan ST
NY, NY 10012

↑ Blue Ribbon

BLUE RIBBON

Just because you can get food at any hour in New York doesn't make it delicious. After a night out, when nothing will do except a raw bar and a New York strip, Blue Ribbon fills that need until 4 a.m. From the beginning, brothers Eric and Bruce Bromberg cultivated after-service industry loyalty and have since spawned a like-minded restaurant empire. The original still satisfies eclectic late-night cravings that might range from restorative matzo-ball soup to a serious rack of lamb.

→ Blue Ribbon

BOULEY

A local icon influenced by the likes of Roger Vergé, David Bouley has in turn instructed some of New York's most respected chefs in American-meets-French fine dining: Dan Barber, Anita Lo, César Ramirez, and Shea Gallante have passed through Bouley's kitchen. Having run downtown restaurants for more than 20 years, Bouley favors an old-fashioned level of opulence. Fresh apples perfume the entryway, which leads to a dining area where gold vaulted ceilings, bustled balloon curtains, and velvet recall the European countryside more than industrial Tribeca. Tasting menus similarly juxtapose the modern (rich porcini flan with black truffle dashi) and the classical (chicken cooked in a pot over hay).

163 Duane ST
NY, NY 10013

➜ Bouley

Burger
Joint
Sun-Thurs.
11 am-11:30 pm
Fri. and Sat.
11 am-midnight

➜ **Burger Joint**

BURGER JOINT

There's a retro snack bar behind heavy curtains at Le Parker Meridien hotel, but thanks to a line into the lobby, it's not too hard to find. Impressively focused, the menu recalls the 1970s *Saturday Night Live* sketch in which John Belushi pushes limited items on diner customers, mainly: "Cheeseburger! Cheeseburger! Cheeseburger!" Here, you can add matchstick fries. Handwritten signs above the counter streamline communication with instructions on how to personalize a burger in three steps and cash-only warnings. Such efficiency is part of the charm.

→ **Burger Joint**

CHEF'S TABLE AT BROOKLYN FARE

Expanding on the idea of an exclusive chef's table, César Ramirez lords over an open metal kitchen that seats 18 guests and has become one of Brooklyn's most sought-after reservations. The austerity of the unique setting turns all attention toward Ramirez's meticulous and ingenious food. With help from a few sous-chefs, he plates more than 20 French-Japanese bites per meal. His menu changes nightly but often highlights pristine seafood, both raw and cooked.

200 Schermerhorn ST
Brooklyn, NY 11201

→ Chef's Table at Brooklyn Fare

CORTON

Restaurateur Drew Nieporent and chef Paul Liebrandt have turned a symbiotic partnership into a contemporary expression of haute gastronomy. This restaurant served as a happy ending to an HBO documentary called *A Matter of Taste*, which followed Liebrandt's search for a project that would support his avant-garde culinary whims. Nieporent provides the artistic chef with a simple, serene canvas for experimentation. The menu changes often, and brilliance always appears in surprising ways, like a salad called From the Garden in which nearly 20 different vegetables seem to grow from the plate.

60 East 65th ST
NY, NY 10065

→ Daniel

60 East 65th ST
NY, NY 10065

→ Daniel

DANIEL

"I am first and foremost born out of tradition in cooking, and I think I inspire myself through tradition," says Daniel Boulud. At the pinnacle of his New York-centric empire, Boulud balances innovation with history. Here, he serves oysters in seawater gelée and pressed duck in a style that dates back to the 19th century at La Tour d'Argent. You will have to order the bird in advance. Boulud finds the perfect local duck and marinates it for at least a week in port wine, orange, and spice to create a sweet glaze while roasting. The sauce is finished, in a proper tableside flourish, with blood extracted by a traditional press.

→ Daniel

85 Tenth AV
NY, NY 10011

➜ Del Posto

DEL POSTO

For Italian through the prism of haute cuisine, the influential trio of Mario Batali, Joe Bastianich, and Bastianich's mother, Lidia Bastianich, erected a proud flagship in an impressively cavernous piece of Manhattan real estate. Their chef, Mark Ladner, takes a studied approach to opulence. Black-truffle butter glazes a single tortello, concealing pungent Puzzone cheese. One-hundred-layer lasagna arrives on its side, cut like a bar of gold. Meanwhile, punk-rock drummer turned pastry chef Brooks Headley skips jarring notes when transitioning into dessert. To avoid a glut of sugar, he coaxes sweetness from vegetables as in celery sorbetto with a sweet-tart agrodolce and goat-cheese globes.

85 Tenth AV
NY, NY 10011

→ Del Posto

2127 Broadway
NY, NY 10023

FAIRWAY
"LIKE NO OTHER MARKET"
WWW.FAIRWAYMARKET.COM

FAIRWAY
"LIKE NO OTHER MARKET"
WWW.FAIRWAYMARKET.COM

FAIRWAY
"LIKE NO OTHER MARKET"
WWW.FAIRWAYMARKET.COM

CANADA DRY

Make your move!
CANADA DRY
Ginger Ale

→ Fairway

FAIRWAY

Sheer variety characterizes this New York super-
market. The Glickberg family grew a Depression-era
fruit cart into a 24,000-square-foot institution
with additional locations, each larger than the
next. Produce still lines the sidewalk, the bakery produces breads and cakes from scratch, and
the store's two floors consist of mind-bogglingly
packed displays, such as a massive meat-and-cheese
case. Taking a shopping cart means having to hold
your own in the sole rickety elevator, vying for
coveted space with Fairway pros.

→ Fairway

99 East 52nd ST
NY, NY 10022

↑ Four Seasons Restaurant (The)

THE FOUR SEASONS RESTAURANT

At the Four Seasons Restaurant (not to be confused with the hotel a few blocks north), owner Julian Niccolini governs midtown's power lunch set. In these magnificent surroundings, you truly feel as though you've arrived. The clientele remains as imposing as the Grill Room itself, where John F. Kennedy once celebrated his 45th birthday. In the aristocratic Pool Room, flowering trees frame a low marble basin that doesn't obstruct views across the monumental space. It's fitting that the renowned architects Mies van der Rohe and Philip Johnson (the man behind Connecticut's Glass House) designed a restaurant where everyone can watch one another.

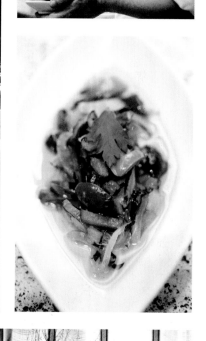

↑ Four Seasons Restaurant (The)

→ Gotham Bar and Grill

GOTHAM BAR AND GRILL

Opened in 1984, this stately restaurant is where chef-partner Alfred Portale introduced skyscraper cuisine. Lemony poached Japanese octopus, scallops, lobster, and flying fish roe still rise in a vertical arrangement for his seafood salad with support from an avocado foundation. Winks to an earlier style aside, Gotham feels very New York with its dignified space framed by city-centric photographs. Portale's menu appeals to newer generations with pork chops and cold-smoked trout with pumpernickel croutons.

↑ **Gotham Bar and Grill**

↑ Gramercy Tavern

GRAMERCY TAVERN

"The restaurant has evolved by pulling talented people from around the world to come and work here. In a way, that describes what makes it distinctly American. The menu changes according to the arrival of ingredients in the market as well as the flow of ideas through the kitchen. It's the kind of food I'd like people to feel drawn to but also comfortable eating frequently. Our pastry chef, Nancy Olson, captures a sense of home baking: the peanut-butter semifreddo takes iconic American flavors and puts them together in a serious but fun way, and her use of fruits, caramels, and salt is really incredible. There's something uniquely warm about eating at Gramercy Tavern. This might be one of the purest expressions of Danny Meyer." —Michael Anthony

1291 Third AV
NY, NY 10021

→ J.G. Melon

TURKEY BURGER	9.50
MOZZARELLA IN CAROZZA	9.00
BREAST OF TURKEY SANDWICH	10.25
GRILLED BREAST OF CHICKEN SANDWICH	10.25
ROAST BEEF SANDWICH	9.95
TURKEY CLUB SANDWICH	11.50
BACON, LETTUCE & TOMATO	9.50
GRILLED CHEESE, TOMATO & BACON	10.25
OMELETTES	10.50
COTTAGE FRIED POTATOES	4.75

SALADS

WARM SLICED CHICKEN SALAD	13.75
CHEF'S SALAD	13.75
SALAD NICOISE	18.75
CHICKEN SALAD	13.75
SPINACH SALAD, MUSHROOMS, FETA CHEESE	10.25
SMALL SPINACH SALAD, BACON & MUSHROOMS	6.50
TOSSED GREEN SALAD	6.25

ENTREES

BROILED FISH OF THE DAY, RICE & SALAD	P/A
ROAST ROCK CORNISH HEN, POTATO & SALAD	16.95
CHOPPED STEAK, POTATO & SALAD	17.25
SMALL SIRLOIN STEAK, POTATO & SALAD	26.00
LARGE SIRLOIN STEAK, POTATO & SALAD	28.25
STEAK TARTARE	19.25

DESSERTS

CHEESE CAKE	7.00
CHOCOLATE CHIP CAKE	7.00
APPLE SOUR CREAM WALNUT PIE	7.00
PECAN PIE	6.50
SEASONAL FRUIT PIE	6.50
KEY LIME PIE	6.50
COFFEE/TEA	2.75

NO CREDIT CARDS

J.G. MELON

The bar burger standard — a mound of judicially packed beef delivered by white bun — has always been this pub's draw, but not as long as you might think. Melon opened in 1972 with the look of an old-timey Irish saloon and some watermelon-themed kitsch mixed in. With meat and beer must come potatoes; here they're cottage fries, sliced like ruffled coins and easy to eat like chips.

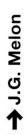

↑ J.G. Melon

↑ Jean Georges

1 Central Park West
NY, NY 10023

JEAN GEORGES

While cooking French food in Bangkok, Singapore, and Japan in the 1980s, Jean-Georges Vongerichten became captivated by Asian ingredients and spices. After landing in New York, he went on to transform fine dining with the notion that an aromatic broth balancing heat and acid can be as accomplished as a rich sauce. The tall windowed space on Central Park impresses while you taste the essential flavors of his work, such as cod enveloped by lemongrass and kaffir lime, or gingery shiitake mushrooms with licorice-braised sweetbreads.

↑ Jean Georges

MAIL ORDER D
SEND A SALAM
THATS ALL
Send a Salami
Your Boy in the Army
KATZ'S DELICATESSEN
ESTABLISHED 1888
NEW YORK CITY
(800) 4 HOTDOG

205 East Houston ST
NY, NY 10002

→ Katz's Delicatessen

KATZ'S DELICATESSEN

Pastrami on rye might be as important to New York's culinary heritage as thin-crust pizza, but old-fashioned cured beef doesn't pop up on every corner. Luckily, there's still Katz's. The best Jewish-style deli also happens to be the oldest, hand-carving pastrami and corned beef since 1888. Staff pile slices of caraway-seeded rye with meat that's been cured for a month. Almost as famous as the gigantic sandwiches: the table immortalized by Meg Ryan in a fit of faux-ecstasy for the 1989 classic *When Harry Met Sally*.

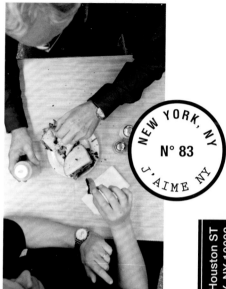

CASH
AND
TRAVELERS
CHECKS
ONLY

→ Katz's Delicatessen

→ Keens

KEENS

Manly storied restaurants seem to have a thing about sticking artifacts on the ceiling. At '21' Club, it's branded toys, and at Keens, you'll notice a vast collection of long-stemmed churchwarden pipes. They came from a pipe club that counted Babe Ruth and Albert Einstein among its members. Founded as a gentlemen's chophouse in 1885 when Herald Square was a theater district, the steakhouse became co-ed 20 years later after actress Lillie Langtry took the men to court. Aged beef is always appropriate, but the "mutton chop" — no longer sheep, but a bone-in saddle of lamb — is a local favorite.

72 West 36th ST

→ Keens

KING COLE BAR

Along with such illustrious guests as Ernest Hemingway, Salvador Dalí, and Marilyn Monroe, the St. Regis Hotel has hosted Old King Cole since 1932. This nursery-rhyme royalty smirks from behind the bar in a 30-foot mural painted by Maxfield Parrish in 1906. Hemingway also frequented Harry's New York Bar in Paris where one of King Cole's first bartenders, Fernand Petiot, worked prior to coming to New York. It was upon his arrival at the St. Regis that Petiot perfected a cocktail called the Red Snapper, combining vodka, tomato juice, Worcestershire sauce, spices, and lemon. Now known worldwide as a Bloody Mary, the original recipe endures as King Cole Bar's signature drink.

→ King Cole Bar

LA GRENOUILLE

Charles Masson carries on his parents' legacy by maintaining the elegance of the French restaurant they opened in 1962. The beauty of those flowers comes from his eye for art and design, a career path he considered before taking over the family business. Masson understands how to get the lighting just so and how to reconcile old and new French classics: frogs' legs Provençale, braised oxtails. This restaurant represents a disappearing way to dine out and is still as welcome as an expert chocolate soufflé.

→ La Grenouille

155 West 51st ST
NY NY 10019

↑ Le Bernardin

155 West 51st ST
NY, NY 10019

LE BERNARDIN

"If you believe that cooking is artistry, you're inspired by your surroundings. Living in a city like New York, you encounter different cultures and ethnicities. You travel, see other things, and then you bring back ingredients, flavors, ideas," explains chef and seafood scholar Eric Ripert, who with supreme hostess Maguy Le Coze, forms one of the most dynamic restaurant partnerships in the United States. This is Maguy's house, with everything exquisitely in its place. Meanwhile, the menu changes constantly, following the mantra that the fish is the star of the plate. "It's powerful because you don't cook with fish. You don't decide, 'I'm going to make that sauce' and scratch your head about what to put with it. You say, 'I have tuna. What can I do to make the tuna better?'" says Ripert.

↑ Le Bernardin

151 East 58th ST
NY, NY 10022

→ Le Cirque

LE CIRQUE

Sirio Maccioni is as much of a legend as his flagship, which opened in 1974 and dazzled celebrities ranging from Henry Kissinger to Jackie Kennedy Onassis — one of the ladies who lunched. While the master of ceremonies entertained his esteemed guests, great chefs like Alain Sailhac, Daniel Boulud, Sylvain Portay, and chocolate whiz Jacques Torres evolved into the mentors of today. Under a dome of curtains conceived by celebrated interior designer Adam Tihany to resemble the big top, some patrons dine on classic Dover sole meunière while others sample newer dishes prepared by the latest chef.

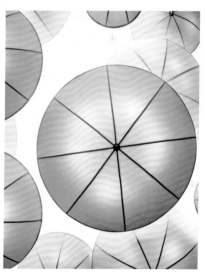

Le Cirque

377 Greenwich ST
NY, NY 10013

→ Locanda Verde

377 Greenwich ST
NY NY 10013

LOCANDA VERDE

Urban Italian is chef Andrew Carmellini's first cookbook with writer and wife Gwen Hyman, and the title captures the essence of this boisterous restaurant co-owned by actor Robert De Niro. It's annexed to De Niro's chic Greenwich Hotel, which attracts movie stars and musicians, and Carmellini updates familiar dishes with new and seasonal ingredient combinations. A signature crostini comes with blue crab and jalapeño. For his Sunday Night Ragu, the chef imports big pasta tubes from Naples and makes a complex sauce of pork ribs, pork shoulder, tomatoes, and browned fennel seed. Pastry chef Karen DeMasco similarly elevates beloved desserts: she pairs her chocolate budino with coffee-crème fraîche gelato, hot fudge, and coffee granita. On weekday mornings, Locanda is a mellower place for a cappuccino and DeMasco's wonderful breakfast breads.

→ Locanda Verde

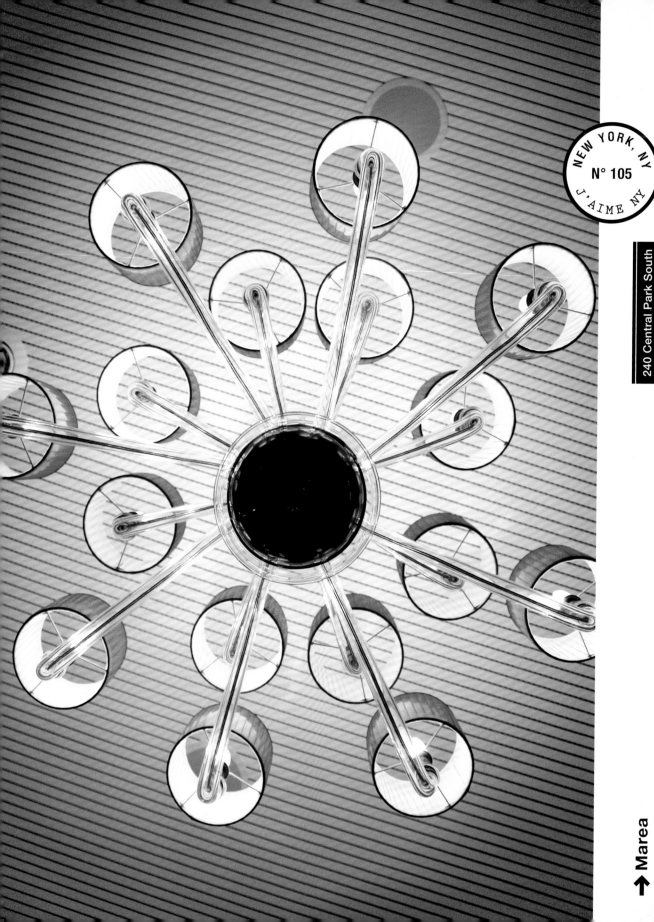

240 Central Park South
NY, NY 10019

➔ **Marea**

240 Central Park South
NY, NY 10019

MAREA

A substantial Midwesterner in size and charisma, Michael White earned his culinary alter ego, Chef Bianco, while training at Ristorante San Domenico in Imola, Italy. He has a talent for pasta. At this luxurious seafood-focused flagship, fantastic crudo, shell sculptures, and pearlescent surfaces still lead to White's ultrarich primi. The many shapes and strands are all made in-house and are exceptional. White emulsifies bone marrow in order to sauce fusilli with red-wine-braised octopus and tops tagliatelle with the freshest crustaceans available worldwide.

➡ Marea

→ Minetta Tavern

MINETTA TAVERN

The master of timeworn spaces, Keith McNally, restored a corner establishment from the 1930s. He kept the old wood paneling plus original photos and caricatures of past regulars. As a Village watering hole, Minetta Tavern never aspired to have food so good. Restaurant partners and Balthazar chefs Lee Hanson and Riad Nasr age beautifully marbled beef for a colossal côte de boeuf served with roasted marrow bones and for the lavish Black Label burger covered in caramelized onions. Their bistro-leaning menu does offer more delicate selections such as fennel-scented dorade, but in such a storied New York clubhouse, you really ought to order a Manhattan cocktail and a steak.

Minetta Tavern

60 East 54th ST
NY, NY 10022

→ **Monkey Bar**

MONKEY BAR

"I went to Monkey Bar when I first came to New York in the 1970s. It always had a slightly raffish air to it," remembers *Vanity Fair* editor-cum-restaurateur Graydon Carter. Opened in the 1930s, the Hotel Elysée's bar earned a nickname as the "easy lay" since lovers often went upstairs. Regulars included media types and writers like Dorothy Parker and Tennessee Williams, who tragically choked to death in his room. To revive Monkey Bar as a restaurant, Carter enlisted industry notables Ken Friedman of the Spotted Pig, former Craft chef Damon Wise, wine-savvy general manager Belinda Chang, and cocktail expert Julie Reiner. "Wise's remit was to do an updated version of classic American fare," says Carter, whose personal contribution to the space is a mural of great New Yorkers from the Jazz Age to the 1940s by illustrator Edward Sorel. "The nice thing about murals is that they tell the story of the restaurant back to you and tell the story of the city back to you. Ed was 82, and getting him to do this was sort of an accomplishment; he can be quite cranky," admits Carter.

60 East 54th ST
NY, NY 10022

→ Monkey Bar

105 Hudson ST
NY, NY 10013

→ Nobu

NOBU

Nobu Matsuhisa's Tribeca restaurant spawned Japanese-fusion branches in more than 20 cities around the world, each with the same level of impeccable talent and quality. Architect David Rockwell, driven by his fascination with theater, designed the original with thematic Eastern elements like birch trees and river stones that offset the pulse of the crowd. Signature miso-glazed black cod balances buttery umami flavor with silky, delicately cooked fish. Other popular dishes, such as ceviche-like Tiradito Nobu-Style, show how the chef was influenced by stints in South America.

105 Hudson ST
NY, NY 100__

→ Nobu

178 Broadway

→ Peter Luger

PETER LUGER

You've come for steak, the focus of this great American tavern since 1887. That's the understanding between patrons and gruff bow-tied waiters who are as likely to tell you your order as they are to take it. Do you want a porterhouse for two, three, or four? Those are the only real options, plus some fried potatoes and maybe a side of buttery creamed spinach. Big plates of dry-aged beef arrive perfectly medium rare and broiled to a char in all the right places. Just don't be surprised when your meat arrives sliced. That's Luger's style and you won't want it any other way.

→ Peter Luger

1 West 59th ST, Concourse Level
NY, NY 10019

➜ Plaza Food Hall by Todd English (The)

THE PLAZA FOOD HALL BY TODD ENGLISH

Founded in 1907, the famous Plaza Hotel now features a fairly modern dining concept on its lower level. Chef Todd English designed eight stations where cooks prepare everything from sushi to sliders, and you can order from all of them at once. English's Mediterranean slant comes through in flatbreads topped with fig jam and prosciutto. The Plaza Niçoise features olive-oil-poached tuna with black-olive vinaigrette.

BURGERS & SLIDERS

THE CLASSIC BURGER
THE FOOD HALL BURGER
TODD BURGER
FALAFEL
CRAB SALAD ROLLS

TB SLIDERS
TURKEY SLIDERS
PRIME RIB SLIDERS
MINI LAMB GYROS
BIG PASTRAMI

CHAR GRILLED

CHORIZO
CHICKEN BREAST
PIEDMONTESE RIB EYE
SWEET-SPICY
BABY BACK RIBS

all served w/pickled veggies,
condiments/choice of bread

CARVERY

Apple Wood Smoked
TURKEY BREAST

ORGANIC
HALF CHICKEN

American

Berber Smoked
PORK SHOULDER

ROASTED
PRIME RIB

Horse
Smoked Kobe Pastrami

1 West 59th ST, Concourse Level
NY NY 10019

→ Plaza Food Hall by Todd English (The)

227 Tenth AV
NY, NY 11011

➜ Red Cat (The)

THE RED CAT

Jimmy Bradley's projects epitomize the American bistro: a lively neighborhood spot that's always a good option, borrows from France and the Mediterranean, and definitely serves roast chicken. Surrounded by West Chelsea's galleries, the restaurant displays local artwork, and guests of nearby openings step into the bar for impromptu dinners and well-made cocktails.

227 Tenth AV
NY NY 11011

→ Red Cat (The)

RED ROOS
Harlem

FIRE ~ ALARM

LIFT
PULL

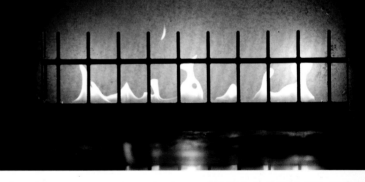

RED ROOSTER

Ethiopian by birth and raised in Sweden (where he also trained in the art of haute cuisine), Marcus Samuelsson put down roots in Harlem. This restaurant is an expression of all these influences. Samuelsson serves his Swedish grandmother's meatballs with lingonberry jam, lentils with coconut rice, and local soul food like fried chicken with gravy and hot sauce. A packed, multicultural crowd underscores how Samuelsson has invigorated the neighborhood's dining scene.

→ Red Rooster

NEVER HIDE

848 Washington ST
NY, NY 10014

→ Standard (The)

Oysters

BLUE POINT
Long Island

FANNY BAY
Washington State

BEAUSOLEIL
New Brunswick

HAMA HAMA
Washington State

WELLFLEET
Massachusetts

YAQUINA
Oregon

THE STANDARD

In an innovative act of urban renewal, abandoned freight-train tracks known as the High Line became an elevated city promenade along the West Side. Appealing to voyeurs inside and out, this hotel from André Balazs straddles the project like an open dollhouse made of concrete and non-reflective glass. Views into the rooms sometimes distract from the glimmering Hudson River. Inside entertainment includes the Standard Grill brasserie on the ground floor, a rooftop lounge unofficially dubbed the Boom Boom Room, and an outpost of Le Bain nightclub, also with panoramic views.

10 Columbus Circle
NY, NY 10019

TIME WARNER CENTER

A deviation from the prototypical American mall, Time Warner Center eschews chain pizza and stir-fry for all-star restaurants. Thomas Keller headlines the fourth floor overlooking Central Park with the most refined fine dining in New York, his tasting-menu-only East Coast flagship Per Se. Across the way, Masayoshi Takayama prepares lavish omakase menus at Masa, and former Windows on the World chef Michael Lomonaco runs the steakhouse Porter House New York. Down a flight, Missy Robbins reigns with fresh pastas at A Voce Columbus, Marc Murphy sells retail-priced wines at his upmarket family restaurant Landmarc, and pastry force Sébastien Rouxel develops fantastic takes on American sweets like Oreos at Keller's cafe and takeaway arm, Bouchon Bakery.

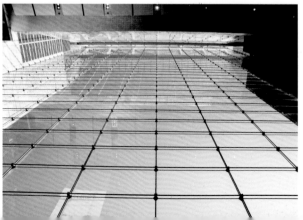

↑ Time Warner Center

10 Columbus Circle
NY, NY 10019

→ Time Warner Center, A Voce

A VOCE

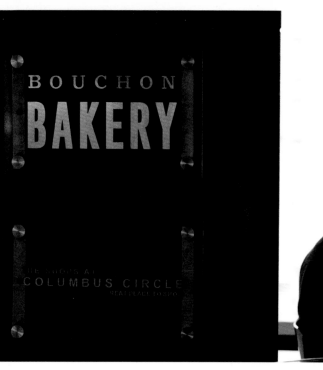

10 Columbus Circle
NY, NY 10019

→ Time Warner Center, Bouchon Bakery

BOUCHON BAKERY

↑ Time Warner Center, Masa

NEW YORK, NY
N° 151
J'AIME NY

10 Columbus Circle
NY, NY 10019

MASA

↑ Time Warner Center, Masa

10 Columbus Circle
NY, NY 10019

↑ Time Warner Center, Per Se

per se

10 Columbus Circle
NY, NY 10019

↑ Time Warner Center, Per Se

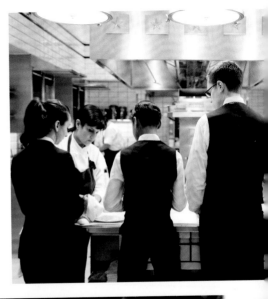

PER SE

"I try to give historical context to each of my restaurants because I want guests to have emotional connections to the food. We focus on ingredients and execution, but some of the things that make our cooking feel more whimsical are takes on familiar American pairings — Coffee and Doughnuts, warm cinnamon doughnuts with cappuccino semifreddo, or Oysters and Pearls, a sabayon of pearl tapioca with oysters and American caviar, which we've been serving for about 17 years. It's the first dish that you're served, and we typically serve it with Champagne. It's rich, luxurious, and celebratory. It's a complete dish, lighthearted and sophisticated." —Thomas Keller

10 Columbus Circle
NY, NY 10019

↑ Time Warner Center, Per Se

PORTER HOUSE NEW YORK

"In a lot of ways, a steakhouse is the most quintessential American restaurant. It's supposed to be fun, a little loud, comfortable, and about great ingredients. It's simple in description, but the elements are very challenging because we spend a good part of every day sourcing beef and seafood. The dry-aged cuts have that nutty, mineral flavor, and we use infrared broilers that reach 1,600 degrees to cook each piece precisely." —Michael Lomonaco

10 Columbus Circle
NY, NY 10019

↑ Time Warner Center, Porter House New York

→ Totonno's Pizzeria Napolitano

TOTONNO'S PIZZERIA NAPOLITANO

Among the forebears of New York pizza, Anthony "Totonno" Pero left America's first official pizzeria, Lombardi's in Manhattan, to open this Coney Island legend in 1924. In keeping with NYC's classic style, these thin-crust pies are coal-fired and as big as hubcaps, dwarfing those puffy, misshapen creations that define the newer artisanal movement. Limited hours of operation are as old-school as the pizzas themselves: Totonno's closes when the dough runs out.

SAUSAGE
MUSHROOM
PEPPERONI
PEPPERS & ONIONS
ANCHOVIES
ONIONS
GARLIC
EXTRA CHEESE

1524 Neptune AV
Brooklyn, NY 11224

→ Totonno's Pizzeria Napolitano

➜ **WD~50**

WD ~ 50

Wylie Dufresne belongs to the scientific school of chefs who are fascinated by the ways that food can be prepared and cooked, and dedicated to advancing techniques. Though this style of cuisine is generally known as molecular gastronomy, key practitioners dismiss that term. Instead, it's about experimentation. Dufresne's research has led to such wonders as eggs Benedict presented as yolk cylinders with deep-fried hollandaise and aerated foie gras with plum, pickled beets, and brioche crisps. His curiosity means there will be something new and exciting to sample every time you return.

↑ WD~50

UR
BAN
PASTO
RAL

35 East 18th ST
NY, NY 10003

→ ABC Kitchen

ABC KITCHEN

Jean-Georges Vongerichten says he and Dan Kluger, the chef at this eco-chic annex to ABC's monumental home store, met over vegetables in Union Square and "became market friends." Both know how to bring out intense seasonal flavors. Crab toast arrives on sourdough with garlic-lemon aioli and gets its kick from green chili. Carrots are roasted whole with thyme, cumin, and dried red chili for a salad with avocado, sprouts, sour cream, and citrus dressing. Vongerichten explains, "I like chilies, Thai chilies, jalapeños. I'm using a bit of bite everywhere. It's about creating that craving."

URBAN PASTORAL
N° 173
J'AIME NY

35 East 18th ST
NY, NY 10003

→ ABC Kitchen

36 East 7th Street

abraço
espresso

tuesday - Saturday
8am - 6pm

Sunday
9am - 6pm

CLOSED MONDAY

SANITARY INSPECTION GRADE

A

NYC

URBAN PASTORAL

N° 175

J'AIME NY

86 East 7th ST
NY, NY 10003

→ Abraço Espresso

ABRAÇO ESPRESSO

Favored by chefs and other food industry types, Abraço is a tiny place that serves intensely concentrated coffee and inventive sweet-savory snacks. Co-owner Jamie Mc-Cormick often pulls espresso shots himself while conversing with walk-ins about everything from restaurants to records. Partner Elizabeth Quijada makes the crumbly loaf cakes, sandwiches, and small plates with ingredients from the Union Square Greenmarket. Since the standing room inside is so constrained, regulars move out to the sidewalk counter to linger over black-olive shortbread cookies and high-octane drinks.

86 East 7th ST
NY, NY 10003

➜ Abraço Espresso

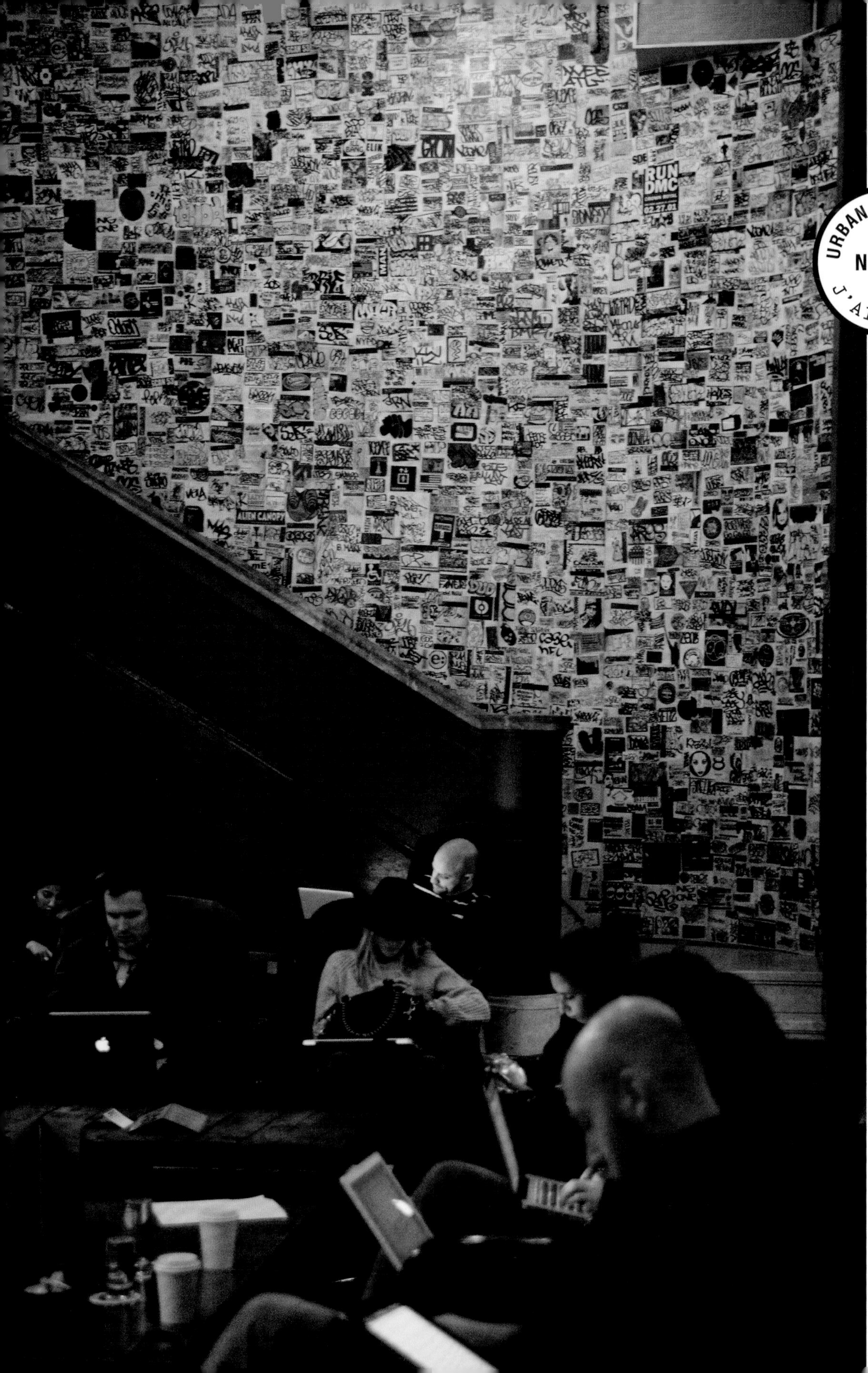

URBAN PASTORAL
N° 179
J'AIME NY

20 West 29th ST
NY, NY 10001

→ Ace Hotel

ACE HOTEL

"We liked the aesthetic and the independence of Alex Calderwood's hotels. He was very like-minded to Ken Friedman and me. It took awhile to get the Breslin up and running, and then the space next door was being built out for the John Dory Oyster Bar. This one was on a corner; it had great windows. We wanted it to be light and airy instead of dark and moody like the Breslin. It's just really nice to sit there with a hot chowder and a buttery Parker House roll and people-watch. Stumptown was an independent coffee company, so we were all really excited to have that brand in the hotel. I think, without sounding too pompous, that we definitely turned the hotel-restaurant concept a little bit on its head. We made it exciting — probably more Ken than me because he has a more bubbly personality." —April Bloomfield

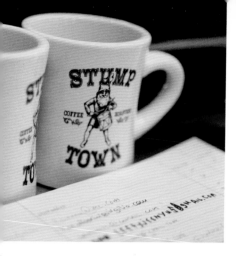

➜ Ace Hotel

BRESLIN

URBAN PASTORAL

N° 183

J'AIME NY

16 West 29th ST
NY, NY 10001

➜ Ace Hotel, Breslin (The)

16 West 29th ST
NY, NY 10001

➔ Ace Hotel, Breslin (The)

THE BRESLIN

1196 Broadway
NY, NY 10001

→ Ace Hotel, John Dory Oyster Bar (The)

1196 Broadway
NY NY 10001

Ace Hotel, John Dory Oyster Bar (The)

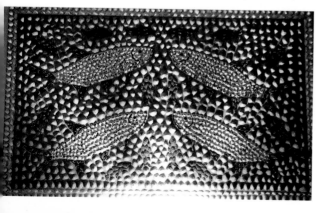

THE JOHN DORY
OYSTER BAR

ALDEA

David Bouley protégé George Mendes weaves the flavors of Portugal and Spain into sophisticated dishes at this minimalist bi-level restaurant. Ingredients like garlic, onion, tomato, bay leaf, and paprika add what Mendes likes to refer to as "gutsy" seasoning to signatures like seared Shrimp Alhinho with pimento. His arroz de pato, duck confit rice with chorizo and olives, is well balanced in texture and taste.

URBAN PASTORAL
N° 191
J'AIME NY

31 West 17th ST
NY, NY 10011

→ Aldea

ARDESIA

With 35 wines by the glass from the Old and New Worlds, it can be hard to commit. So owner Mandy Oser promises that you'll always be offered a taste of that Grüner Veltliner or Pinot Noir from California's Anderson Valley. Chef Amorette Casaus emphasizes small plates. Maybe you'll start with a crostino of house goat's-milk ricotta. Casaus also makes cocktail sausages with smoked pork jowl and street-vendor-style pretzels with spicy mustard and Gruyère cheese sauce. Meanwhile, servers retrieve bottles from the two-story wine wall via metal catwalk, a reference to the scaffolding present throughout this developing neighborhood.

229 Bedford AV
Brooklyn, NY 11211

→ Bedford Cheese Shop

Berkswell $35 lb
raw sheep, Ram Hall, Berkswell, w Midlands, England
Stephen Fletcher has created the nuttiest, fullest
sheep cheese I have ever tasted. This is a work
of art. It will leave you begging for more. The
Italians should learn how to make Pecorino
from Stephen.

Montgomery's Cheddar $30 lb
raw cow, north calbury, england
A true farm house cheddar. This mammoth
is made by Michael Chase and the gang, 1¾
wheels are hand selected by folks at Neal's
Yard, and hurled across the pond to our lovely
shop. It will be the best cheddar you will ever
have...ever. Pair with anything remotely
alcoholic and a pot of Branston pickle.

Gruyere (the other one) $30 lb
raw cow, turn, Switzerland
This sweet, toasty, baby shallots just been caramelized
tasting swiss has just found a new home with us. It's
aged 12 months, creamy without the crystals, but still has
mammoth flavors, like the secret weapon of Dirk Diggler;
this bad boy will amaze even the most finicky cheese eater.
Pair with a white jura.

Fricalin hostettler $27 lb
raw cow, Switzerland
What a sweet little kicker this guy is ...one of the
best new swiss cheeses around. If you like Hoch
Ybrig than you'll love the Fricalin. The perfect
treat to spice up mac an' cheese or make any
omelette to die for. Pair with some Pawer's and
a dutch.

Adelegger
cow, italy, germany
7 organic farms formed a cooperative
one cheese. Have you ever had some
mouth that was simultaneously sweet
buttery yet punchy? If not my friend,
out. This incredibly complex cheese is
Washed with white wine and fresh he
month rest, it'll slap you across the fa
you wanting more.

emmenthal   beeler $31 lb
raw cow, emmenthal, Switzerland
...hands down the best emmenthal available. Period.
...t's nutty, rich, and its got holes! From partially
...kimmed milk, it's the closest you'll get to low fat in
...his store. An essential player in any great fondue,
...t's the Condaleeza Rice to our personal Bush
...Administration. Pair with lots and lots of Q... ...lu.les.

Wilde Weide $31 lb
raw cow, holland
Aged 15 months, this organic milk gouda is the
true essence of what fermented cheese should be.
These Hilpard our bovine love the life of luxury
green grass, low fog, lots of love, and they can get
some of the best cannabis known to man. It'll
give you the munchies and inspire you to buy a
farm and settle down... with your favorite brew.

Kw...
...Jack...
...thr...

Booenkaas 20
raw cow, flanders, h...
Remember when...
...is past like that, 1 ...
toffee, peanut b...
sensed like the b...
of yummy won...
will all make s...
a part of Ovea...

Monte Enebro
"Queserías del Tietar, SL,"
LA AIRAIN (avila)   ESPAÑA
E 15.00758AV   C.E.E.
23-12-3024   HT DM

BEDFORD CHEESE SHOP

Befriending cheesemongers is one way to cultivate a neigh-borhood feel within the grand scheme of the city. Jangling open the door releases that wonderful funk of a proper fromagerie. Point and sample, and dairy buffs will deci-pher your tastes. Owner Charlotte Kamin sources rounds of Piedmontese La Tur, Morbier from the Jura, hunks of Australian feta, and Salvatore Bklyn ricotta made in town with milk from upstate. Her sundries set off pantry fan-tasies. Imported specialties like Rustichella d'Abruzzo pasta and Dijon mustards share space with goods produced nearby, such as Sour Puss Pickles, Mázi Piri Piri hot sauce, and s'mores candies from Tumbador Chocolate.

BEDFORD CHEESE SHOP 2

FARMSTEAD

229 Bedford AV
Brooklyn, NY 11211

Perazola
cow, asturias, spain
Oh boy, oh boy! It's a full flavored, piquant
from the rugged, masculine coast of Spain's
region of Asturias. It's a weathered, sailor's
these cheese makers. All barrels of rum and
sweaty nights huddled close together in dark
corridors. As for the cheese, it's blue and bitin
pretty damn good for a cheese made by water
folk. Pair as with a

sheep's coming out of the is
does make the journey acros
o us all. This incredible, smo
a firmness that betrays it's other-
he taste of fresh fields and morning
very bite. Eat alone and savor the

→ **Bedford Cheese Shop**

↑ Blue Hill at Stone Barns

BLUE HILL AT STONE BARNS

"We think about recipes from the ground up, literally, so it's not just about the flavors of a leg of lamb or a carrot when it's in the kitchen, but from the moment it's born or first appears in the field. The lamb that we serve is raised on all grass. When you put an animal on a pasture, it roams around eating the best grass at the best time. That's probably the definition of sustainability: allowing the lamb to eat what it wants or the carrot to take in what the soil is able to produce. But it's always shocking to me that the best choices for ecological farming are always the best flavor choices. That's a nice way to be a chef because it's very connected to a larger system that works, which is nature."
—Dan Barber

630 Bedford RD
Tarrytown, NY 10591

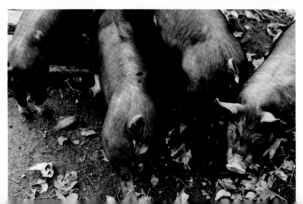

Blue Hill at Stone Barns

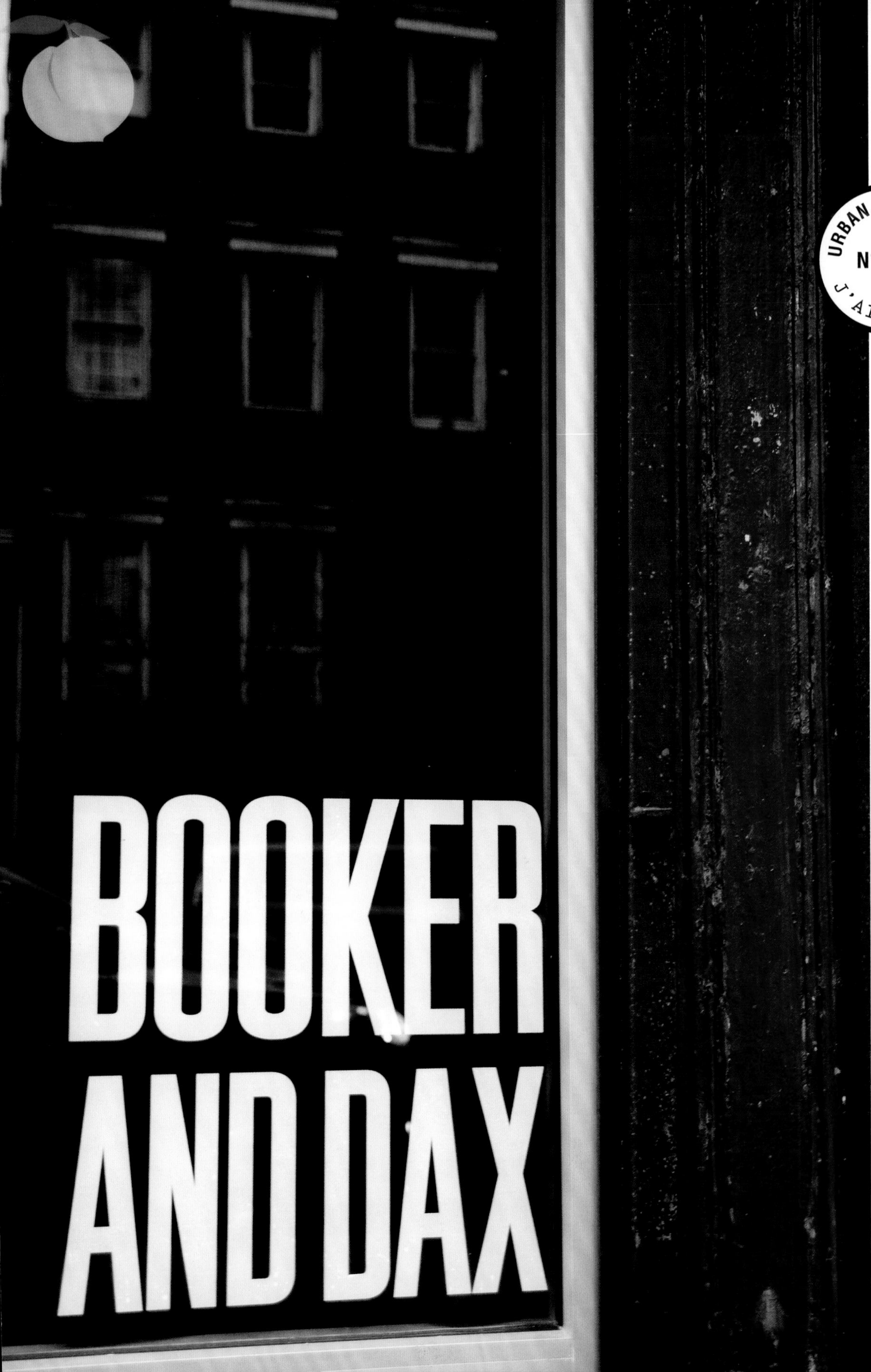

207 2nd AV
NY, NY 10003

BOOKER
AND DAX

➜ Booker and Dax

BOOKER AND DAX

Momofuku's David Chang partnered with the French Culinary Institute's director of culinary technology, Dave Arnold, on this advanced cocktail bar where liquid nitrogen and hot pokers are the new shakers and stirrers. Arnold trains his mixologists to chill glassware with the former while the Red Hot Poker heats individual drinks and caramelizes their sugars — as in the well-named Friend of the Devil with sweet vermouth, Campari, rye whiskey, and Pernod.

↑ Booker and Dax

I don
Hot
I ha
privat
i
T

Yo
Say
a B
a
Lik
a
T

↑ Broadway Panhandler

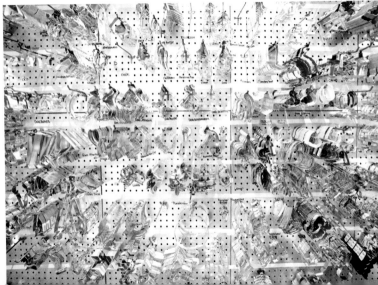

65 East 8th ST
NY, NY 10003

BROADWAY PANHANDLER

As this store's name suggests, there are pans everywhere, hundreds according to proprietor Norman Kornbleuth: All-Clad sauteuses, Bourgeat copper cookware, Le Creuset casseroles above and below. Intrigued when culinary icon James Beard went shopping in his father's restaurant supply store, Kornbleuth envisioned and later realized a retail shop that would bring industry tools to home cooks. Beyond pans, customers come for cutlery (nearly 30 chef's knives alone), bakeware, and kitchen requisites as simple as a great peeler.

→ Broadway Panhandler

79 North 11th ST
Brooklyn, NY 11211

↑ Brooklyn Brewery

BROOKLYN BREWERY

Founded in 1987, Steve Hindy's brewery now represents Brooklyn's artisanal force with a production facility in the center of Williamsburg. Peerless brewmaster Garrett Oliver, editor-in-chief of *The Oxford Companion to Beer*, oversees core styles like Brooklyn Lager, seasonal brews, and reserve editions like Sorachi Ace made with a single-hop variety of the same name. Those who want to sample from the source can visit the factory during Friday-night happy hour, when staff let you order delivery to picnic tables in the tasting room.

79 North 11th ST
Brooklyn NY 11011

➜ Brooklyn Brewery

East River Waterfront, N 6 and 7th ST

→ Brooklyn Flea/Smorgasburg

ICE
CREAM
SAND-
WICHE
& COOKIES

$4

IVORY LENTILS

BLACK-EYED PEAS

MAYACOBA

RED CHIEF

I 8 NY
#1 Roasted $6
   Chicken
 -salsa verde,
  Pickled green
  tomato
#2 Ricotta $6
 -grilled eggplant,
 empress plums, mint.
Grilled Corn
 -smoked apple
  butter $4
Lemon verbena

East River Waterfront, N 6 and 7th ST
Brooklyn, NY 11211

BROOKLYN FLEA/ SMORGASBURG

Here, you'll find the newest artisanal food products. Masterminds Eric Demby and Jonathan But-
ler adopted the concept of a weekend flea market
to create a demand for limited-edition edibles.
Now, Brooklyn Flea's offshoot, Smorgasburg, sells
food from more than 100 vendors. Headlining the
swarmed buffet: Solber Pupusas griddles El Salva-
dorian corn cakes; AsiaDog tops beef, chicken, or
vegetarian wieners with surprising condiments like
sesame slaw; and Pizza Moto turns out pies from a
brick-oven trailer. The flea's blog teases weekly
newcomers. After a lobster roll one week, you might
return the next for Thai food, fresh watermelon
soda, and wild blueberry preserves to take home.

↑ Brooklyn Flea/Smorgasburg

CIANO

Gnocchi, cavatelli, ravioli — chef Shea Gallante rolls and pinches 10 to 20 varieties of fresh pasta in any given season. The setting is warm and somewhat Tuscan, but Gallante counters the rusticity with a highbrow menu. He dresses cortecce — like a stretched orecchiette — with braised octopus, pancetta, red onion, and bread crumbs, and uses duck in a rich Bolognese. John Slover's wine program lets you open and buy just half of certain bottles on his Italian-leaning list.

↑ Ciano

↑ **Craft**

CRAFT

"I looked at what I had been doing over the last 20 years, and I realized that every season my food was starting to become simpler. I thought, 'What would it look like 20 years from now? Why can't I do a restaurant with sea bass, just pan-roasted with salt and pepper and olive oil, and a perfect plate of morels?' If I thought I would have had that much influence, I think I would have been afraid to do it. When Craft started in 2001, a lot of people were confused by it. You order a main; you order some sides. It really gives you the chance to evoke the seasons. Ingredients that come out of the ground at the same time have a natural affinity for each other." —Tom Colicchio

43 East 19th ST
NY, NY 10003

→ Craft

CRUSH WINE & SPIRITS

Robert Schagrin considers the four pillars of Crush's offerings to be the regions of Champagne, Germany/Austria, Piedmont, and Burgundy, which accounts for approximately 1,000 of the selections. Besides desirable acquisitions from private cellars (with marks of proper aging like "beautiful fills and spinning capsules"), eclectic wines are a point of pride — such as bottles of Huet Vouvray dating back to 1945 and aged Vin Jaunes from the Jura. Schagrin chose vinification materials like glass, steel, and stone for the striking design of the shop, opened with partners Drew Nieporent and Josh Guberman. Toward the back, "The Cube," a temperature-controlled glass room, holds extra-nice bottles that you're welcome to browse.

↑ Crush Wine & Spirits

623 Eleventh AV
NY, NY 10036

Take-Out & Catering for All Occasions

Daisy May's
BBQ
USA

Corner of 46th St. 11th Ave.
N.Y.C.
(212) 977-1500

→ Daisy May's BBQ USA

DAISY MAY'S
BBQ USA

623 Eleventh AV
NY, NY 10036

Grilling authority Adam Perry Lang did turns at Le Cirque, Daniel, and Guy Savoy in Paris before abandoning French fine dining for the pigs. Lang's barbecued pork butt won first place at Kansas City's World Series of Barbecue, and this cafeteria-style Hell's Kitchen joint he founded specializes in pulled-pork sandwiches and Memphis-style dry-rubbed pork ribs. Reserving large cuts requires allies; group diners don latex gloves to attack the most succulent bits of whole animals and butts, all rubbed with spices and cooked for hours in a pit. There will still be leftovers for days on end.

→ Daisy May's BBQ USA

URBAN PASTORAL

N° 231

J'AIME NY

38 Eighth AV
NY, NY 10014

➜ Dell' Anima

DELL' ANIMA

Among the new guard of restaurateurs, chef Gabe Thompson
and Italian wine buff Joe Campanale appeal to young well-
versed diners with powerfully seasoned food and a seamless
beverage program. Thompson chars octopus tentacles until
ultra-tender for a warm salad with beans and chorizo
and makes sausage for a quick, firm risotto alla pilota.
Campanale's list emphasizes small regional producers,
and cocktails — like a sparkling Negroni Sbagliato with
Campari, Carpano Antica, white Lambrusco, and muddled
roasted orange — star house-made ingredients.

THE ART OF CHESS BOXING

→ Dell' Anima

URBAN PASTORAL

N° 235

J'AIME NY

85 Broadway
Brooklyn, NY 11249

→ Diner

DINER

The name Diner might seem like a misnomer, given such a progressive menu of seasonal American food, but Andrew Tarlow's pioneering Williamsburg restaurant does keep diner hours. It opens when others close — in blizzards, during hurricanes, and on the Fourth of July. Servers scribble descriptions of the market-driven dishes on paper lining your table: vibrant salads with raw and roasted elements, fettucine with chanterelles, grass-fed steak. In a continued show of Brooklyn brilliance, this mobbed diner car spawned a gustatory strip. At Marlow & Sons, a general store and restaurant next door, you can order oysters and Champagne or a cappuccino to go in a sustainable cup. Marlow & Daughters, the larder down the block, sells meat butchered from whole farm-raised animals and even bags made with the cow's leather.

85 Broadway
Brooklyn, NY 11249

Diner

103 West 77th ST
NY, NY 10024

↑ Dovetail

DOVETAIL

Most days, diners come for John Fraser's New American
dishes like olive-oil-poached halibut with olives or
sirloin with beef-cheek lasagna. On Monday nights,
he directs your attention to vegetables. Fraser
compares a produce-driven dish to a Rubik's Cube — the
possibilities multiply when meat becomes a condiment.
He might add umami to daikon steaks by glazing them
with miso or deepen the savory components of corn
risotto with beef cap and marrow.

354 Metropolitan AV
Brooklyn, NY 11211

→ Fette Sau

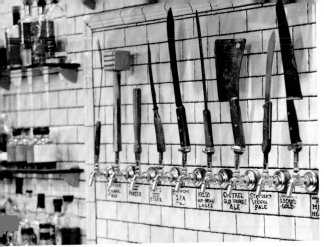

BEEF CHART

ot Round

Round Steak Top Round Bottom

ROUND

RUMP

Rolled Rump   Standing

SIRLOIN

Sirloin Steak   Pin Bone Sirl

GERMAN POTATO SALAD $3⁵⁰/⁷⁵ Lg

CORAS BROCCOLI SALAD $3⁷⁵/⁵⁰

GUSS HALF SOUR PICKLES $1⁵⁰ sm /3 Lg

GUSS SAUERKRAUT $2⁰⁰ sm /3⁷⁵ Lg

NORTH FORK POTATO CHIPS $2⁷⁵

ROUTE 11 HABAÑERO POTATO CH...

SODA

MANHATTAN SPECIAL (8oz BOTTLE) $3⁰⁰

-PURE ESPRESSO -ORANGE -VANILLA CREAM

GOTHAM ARTISINAL (12oz BOTTLE) $3⁰⁰

-CHEERWINE -BUBBLE UP -DAD'S ROOT BEER

-COCK 'N' BULL GINGER BEER $3⁰⁰

-COCA COLA CLASSIC (8 oz BOTTLE) $3⁰⁰

-SWEET LEAF ORGANIC SWEET TEA (16 oz Bottle) $4⁰⁰

-SARATOGA STILL WATER $3⁰⁰

DESSERT

-STEVE'S AUTHENTIC KEY LIME TART $7⁰⁰ (MADE IN RED HOOK)

-NUNU'S CHOCOLATE $8⁰⁰/$12⁰⁰ (MADE IN BROOKLYN)

MONDAY - FRIDAY   5-11pm

SATURDAY & SUNDAY   12-11pm

354 Metropolitan AV
Brooklyn, NY 11211

FETTE SAU

"It's not the easiest thing to turn a mechanic's garage into a restaurant, but it was too good to pass up," says Joe Carroll, who fused barbecue culture (ordering by weight, butcher-paper-lined trays, communal tables) with a signature style of wood-smoked meat. "I wanted to take the technique but do it in a language that spoke to New Yorkers. That's what led us to doing pork belly, pork cheeks, and pastrami," he explains. Drinks include artisanal American whiskey like Pappy Van Winkle and local beers from Kelso and Sixpoint sold in big glass growlers. Considering how much pork stars on the menu, it makes sense that the name means "fat pig" in German (a nod to the European ancestry of his wife and partner, Kim). Here's what you might not know: "It's really what you would call another person. There are older Germans who think it's offensive," he confesses.

→ Fette Sau

FRANNY'S

This is what happens when an advocate for sustainable agriculture (Francine Stephens) marries a chef with a passion for Italian food and pizza (Andrew Feinberg). "The chefs who came to eat wanted to come work with us," says Stephens. Late summer, there's no question that you'll find perfect heirloom tomatoes. Fall might bring sliced pears, sunchokes, and hazelnuts, blanketed by a flurry of Pecorino. Feinberg's star clam pie remains constant, covered in shucked clams with fresh cream, parsley, and dried Sicilian chilies. Stephens focuses on Italian wines made with indigenous varietals: "It's a combination of producers whom I've met and respect for their farming techniques," she says. For dessert, a flawless panna cotta has a supple creaminess that's just right.

→ Franny's

391 Van Brunt ST
Brooklyn, NY 11231

→ Good Fork (The)

THE GOOD FORK

The Red Hook area of Brooklyn has been settled since 1636, so you'd think that this peninsula would have better access to public transportation by now. This homey restaurant from chef Sohui Kim and husband Ben Schneider is a reason to take a car. Kim makes delicate pork-and-chive dumplings and a duck breast with roasted plum and French lentils. Her signature dish is Korean "steak and eggs" over kimchi rice.

→ Good Fork (The)

170 Waverly Place
NY, NY 10014

→ Joseph Leonard

JOSEPH LEONARD

The West Village specializes in small convivial restaurants that neighbors slip into for dinner. Gabe Stulman creates corner gems that attract visitors from other zip codes to wait for a table. This is the buzzy nucleus of his operation, which includes Jeffrey's across the street and a remake of Village landmark Fedora down the block. Once you're in, you can hang out by the zinc bar. It's a homey sort of night out — candlelit with tasty food — that makes diners wish they lived next door.

↑ Joseph Leonard

CHAFING DISH POSSIBILITIES

THE GROCER'S HAND BOOK

VINTAGE MAGAZINE ADS
All originals from 1910's, 1920's
and 1930's — Great kitchen art
A = $18.00
B = $21.00
C = $24.00
A few specials as priced

KITCHEN ARTS & LETTERS

Dedicated to the literature of food, Nach Waxman procures the best selection of new and out-of-print cookbooks, culinary reference guides, and other writings for the scholarly gourmand. Browsing stacks might reveal turn-of-the-century works from Fannie Farmer (who helped standardize America's use of measurements in recipes) or cocktail historian David Wondrich's *Punch: The Delights (and Dangers) of the Flowing Bowl*. Some tomes even come in French. In case you can't pinpoint just the right one in the store, staff will track down hard-to-find titles free of finder's fee and obligation to buy.

→ Kitchen Arts & Letters

90 Bedford ST
NY, NY 10014

↑ Little Owl (The)

THE LITTLE OWL

Chef Joey Campanaro likes to say that "necessity is the mother of all invention." He adapted a seasonal bistro menu to the constraints of a cramped kitchen. He broils fish instead of grilling it and serves his grandmother's meatballs as sliders on wee house-made buns. The iconic pork chop, though, is huge and beautifully grilled. Though often referred to as the consummate neighborhood spot, Little Owl is actually way too busy for casual walk-ins. A place this small requires reservations.

90 Bedford ST

→ Little Owl (The)

URBAN PASTORAL
N° 265
J'AIME NY

93 East 7th ST

→ Luke's Lobster

LUKE'S LOBSTER

There are now several of these Maine seafood shacks tempering the urban landscape with takeout seafood rolls, buoy accents, and fisherman art, thanks to young entrepreneurs Luke Holden and Ben Conniff. Lobster rolls are the main attraction: sweet claw and knuckle meat (shipped down from the Holden family seafood business in Portland) stuffed into toasted buns, with a squiggle of mayo, a drizzle of butter, and a shake of celery-salt-based seasoning. The business model stays consistent via Maine Root organic sodas, state-brewed craft beers, and an enthusiastic vibe from fresh-faced staff.

Now Serving
CRAFT BEER from MAINE

Peeper Ale

ALLAGASH BREWING

GEARY'S

GREAT BREWERS

FEDERAL RESERVE NOTE
THE UNITED STATES OF AMERICA
Welcome to the Room
B 06795150 L
ONE DOLLAR

GIFT CARDS AVAILABLE!

Luke's Lobster   Taste of Maine $22

ner Combo   Soups
l chips, drink   Seafood Chowda $8
7 & pickle   New England Clam Chowda $7
                  Soup of the Day $7   Noah's Ark $41
                                        Great meal for TWO!
available!   1 lobster, 1 crab, 1 shrimp roll
                  Empress Claws 4 for $6   cut in half
Our rolls   Whoopie pies $3   with 4 claws, 2 drinks
remade   Maine Soda $2   & 2 chips
with —   Chips $1
MAYO
UTTER

→ Luke's Lobster

↑ Mile End

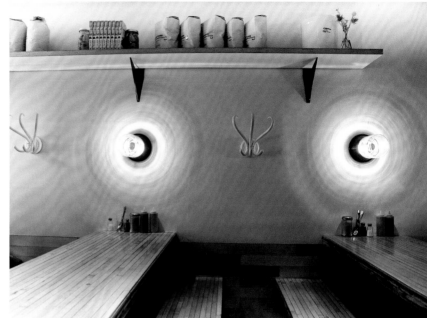

MILE END

Noah Bernamoff and wife Rae Cohen run a Jewish delicatessen
the Montreal way but also the Brooklyn way. There's brisket
smoked in the Canadian tradition, taut bagels driven down
from St-Viateur up north, and that hot mess of fries and
gravy known as poutine. Outer-borough tendencies include
making things like rye bread and sauerkraut from scratch.

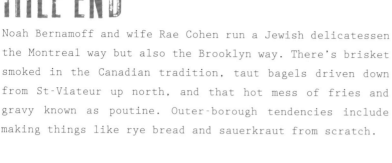

97 Hoyt ST
Brooklyn, NY 11217

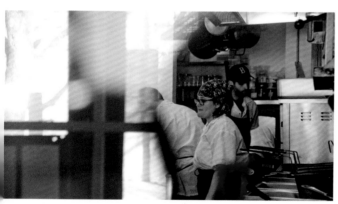

➡ Mile End

207 Second AV
NY, NY 10003

↑ Momofuku Ssäm Bar

MOMOFUKU SSÄM BAR

To think, David Chang began this influential concept as an Asian burrito shop. Then chefs started showing up late night for his strikingly toothsome food flavored with fatty pork, Northeast produce, and pungent Asian ingredients like fish sauce. Chang's after-hours cooking style took over the restaurant, which along with his original Noodle Bar, incited a wave of pork allegiance. Signature pork-belly buns are here — plus chewy rice cakes with spicy sausage ragu, seasonal flashes like chanterelles with pickled quail eggs, and a reservation-only Bo Ssäm pork shoulder that serves six to ten and involves oysters, kimchi, delectable sauces, and lettuce wraps.

→ Momofuku Ssäm Bar

MOTORINO

- ★ -

let us cater
yOur new yeAr's
bALL

*

MAIL YOUR PACKAGES
EARLY, $O THE POst
OFFICE CAN LOSE
THEM IN TIME FOR
XMAS

→ Motorino

MOTORINO

It takes a Belgian to come up with a brussels sprout pizza. Chef Mathieu Palombino defected from fine dining to immerse himself in pizza-craft, and his product is wonderfully original. He acquired top equipment — an Acunto brick oven that climbs to 900 degrees — and sources the best ingredients, perfecting dough that swells and bubbles into a tangy, chewy crust. Most reminiscent of his past, Palombino fires a pie topped with pancetta, house-made fior di latte mozzarella, and that bitter vegetable, which frazzles under the heat. "In every restaurant where I've worked, ladies say they like brussels sprouts," he reasons. The appeal goes beyond his target demographic.

→ Motorino

→ O. Ottomanelli & Sons

O. OTTOMANELLI & SONS

Four Ottomanelli brothers run this butcher shop founded by their father, Onofrio, on Bleecker Street more than 60 years ago. Some customers have been coming for several decades to buy Colorado lamb, house-made pork-and-fennel sausage, and Midwestern beef dry-aged from 14 to 36 days. As a way to stand out when this block was lined with food markets, Onofrio introduced game meats like buffalo, wild boar, and pheasant. During the holidays, venison sausages made with a secret blend of spices go on sale. "My grandparents were butchers in Bari, Italy, and we carried on the tradition," says Frank O., whose son already works in the store.

O. OTTOMANELLI & SONS

THE ORIGINAL
O. Ottomanelli
& SONS
# PRIME MEAT MARKET
TRY OUR HOME MADE SAUSAGE

ITALIAN HOT & SWEET	3.99 Lb
LAMB	
CHICKEN	
VENISON	

NO PRESERVATIVES OR ADDITIVES
STEAKS CUT TO ORDER

PERSONALLY SELECTED --- NATURALLY DRY-AGED

NY SHELL STEAK BONELESS	
BONELESS RIB EYE	
PORTER HOUSE , T-BONE	
NEWPORT STEAK	
BONELESS SIRLOIN STEAK	

285 Bleecker ST
NY, NY 10014

Staten Island Ad...

As a city changes, a business t...

→ O. Ottomanelli & Sons

→ Peasant

PEASANT

"In Italy, I'm most drawn to Puglia, where almost every house had these wood-burning ovens or rotisseries. I used to draw this kitchen for years, and I stockpiled brick left over from building demolitions to build it. I love everything about it. Just because you cook something over a fire, it's not the same effect as smoking it. It's much more subtle than anyone would think. It's about the product and not altering it too much. Suckling pigs come from five or six miles away. The baby hen is simply stuffed with herbs and bread and cooked on the rotisserie. It's all part of the same concept, which is ingredient-driven and minimal. And that's the hardest trick." —Frank DeCarlo

194 Elizabeth ST
NY NY 10012

→ Peasant

PEELS

Breakfast runs until 5 p.m. nightly. Owners William Tigertt and Taavo Somer of Freemans designed an all-day spot for their stylish following, and the menu includes items that will leave you feeling health-conscious or semi-conscious. Making a case for the latter: pastry chef Shuna Lydon's buttery biscuits (topped with poached eggs and sausage gravy), plus cocktails like the Bond St. Swizzle with gin, almondy orgeat syrup, and absinthe. Repentant types return the next day for dainty salads with grilled shrimp or Spa Eggs featuring just the whites.

166 South 4th ST
Brooklyn, NY 11211

Pies 'n' Thighs

PIES 'N' THIGHS

This Southern spot thrives on the happy vibe of customers piling in for fried chicken and chocolate pudding pie. Owners Sarah Buck, Carolyn Bane, and Erika Geldzahler spent two years preparing a new space for the resurrection of a beloved neighborhood hole-in-the-wall that had been forced to close. With its primary colors and mismatched chairs, the front room feels like a country schoolhouse and displays comforting sweets like sugar doughnuts and the namesake dessert. In a lofty brick room out back, patrons eat their biscuits and crunchy thighs in chairs that also recall grade school.

110 East 7th ST
NY, NY 10009

→ Porchetta

PORCHETTA

You've come for pork on a plate or pork in a sandwich,
like chef Sara Jenkins used to eat as a child growing
up in Italy. At her small takeout joint, she seasons
the meat aggressively, in a typical Roman way — with
garlic, sage, rosemary, and wild fennel pollen — and
roasts lean loins with juicy belly and crisping skin.
Jenkins makes a point of including this textural
trilogy in every serving.

110 East 7th ST

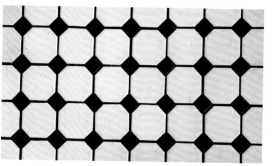

PORSENA

→ Porchetta

PRIME MEATS

New York was always a serious oyster town. In *Appetite City: A Culinary History of New York*, William Grimes describes oysters that "grew as large as dinner plates" in the mid-1800s. The half shells aren't gargantuan here, but restaurateurs Frank Falcinelli and Frank Castronovo serve fantastic Blue Points from Long Island at their turn-of-the-century-style tavern. With its crunchy cabbage salads and house-made sausages, the menu might be considered "Brooklyn local" with a Germanic slant. This explains an exemplary house pretzel: chewy on one end, it narrows to a crisp twist and arrives warm with good butter and strong mustard. Prohibition-inspired cocktails include a daily house punch.

PRUNE

There's no better place to witness the ritual of brunch than this 28-seat restaurant that causes a sidewalk frenzy on weekend mornings. In her memoir, *Blood, Bones & Butter*, chef-owner Gabrielle Hamilton recalls being pregnant and nearly trampled by ravenous fans of her hearty plates: soft-scrambled eggs with smoked bacon, a buttery fried Monte Cristo sandwich. It's more civilized at dinner when Hamilton's love of intensely savory flavors turns up in roasted marrow bones, head-on shrimp with anchovy butter, and spiced lamb shanks.

URBAN PASTORAL

N° 305

J'AIME NY

54 East 1st ST
NY NY 10003

→ Prune

529 Hudson ST
NY, NY 10014

↑ Red Farm

RED FARM

Ed Schoenfeld started his Chinese-food
education as a young New Yorker eating at
Shun Lee and organizing banquets with local
chefs. During reconnaissance in Brooklyn
years later, he discovered chef Joe Ng,
who started mastering the art of dim sum at
age 11 in Kowloon. Their partnership with
restaurateur Jeffrey Chodorow inspired this
project, which emphasizes Ng's dumplings
and local products, hence the bucolic
design. Dim sum fillings range from duck
with crab to crunchy kung pao chicken.
In a flash of humor, Ng shapes har gow
filled with shrimp like the ghosts in Pac-
Man, who appears on the plate as a slice
of deep-fried sweet potato threatening to
chomp before you do.

↑ Red Farm

GARDEN

NO
ACCESS

→ Roberta's

ROBERTA'S

Like a beacon for hipsters from New York to Los Angeles, this barn-style pizzeria with exciting locally driven dishes from chef Carlo Mirarchi has become an archetypal example of Brooklyn's dining culture. California's sustainable-food pioneer Alice Waters awarded Roberta's a small grant for some of its first makeshift outdoor planters, and Heritage Radio Network even broadcasts food shows from a recycled shack in the garden out back. At communal tables, young families devour pizzas like the Axl Rosenberg (sopressata, mushroom, garlic, and jalapeño) next to food obsessives eating lamb belly with goat yogurt. Mirarchi experiments with extended tasting menus that are very difficult to book.

261 Moore ST

PLEASE SHUT THE *DOOR* BEHIND YOU THANKS

FIRE EXTINGUISHER

→ Roberta's

GENUINE NOVA SCOTIA   GENUINE   STUF   N   GREEK

→ Russ & Daughters

RUSS & DAUGHTERS

Recognized by the Smithsonian Institute as a thriving example of Jewish cultural heritage in New York, this gourmet shop specializes in "appetizing" — described as food one eats with bagels — and traces its history back to the early 1900s on the Lower East Side. Family members with four generations of expertise sell an unequaled selection of smoked fish from wild Western Nova salmon to hot-smoked brook trout. It's a classic place to shop or pick up a sandwich covered in cream cheese and your choice of seafood from the case.

↑ Russ & Daughters

378 Metropolitan AV
Brooklyn, NY 11211

➜ Saltie

SALTIE

Loaves of olive-oil cake, currant-filled English pastries, and one sizable Spanish tortilla are on display at this sandwich shop. The team making everything from scratch — Caroline Fidanza, Elizabeth Schula, and Rebecca Collerton — tap many cuisines for inspiration as long as meticulously sourced ingredients combine for a bright, chewy, crunchy lunch, that is, actually, a little bit salty. A loose nautical theme informs the names of each order: The Ship's Biscuit is topped with soft scrambled eggs and ricotta, and the Scuttlebutt consists of hard-boiled eggs, feta, olives, capers, and pickled vegetables on fresh focaccia.

IT'S A TIGHT SHIP

387-4777

HOURS 10-6
CLOSED MONDAYS

↑ Saltie

11 Madison AV
NY, NY 10010

→ Shake Shack

SHAKE SHACK
MADISON SQUARE PARK

Burgers
Our Black Angus burgers are 100% all natural. No hormones and no antibiotics ever. We grind our proprietary Shack blend fresh daily. Our burgers are cooked to medium and served plain unless otherwise requested. Let us know if you would like lettuce, tomato, pickle or onion.

ShackBurger®
American cheese, lettuce, tomato and ShackSauce.
$4.50 Single
$7.00 Double

Hamburger
$3.00 Single
$5.50 Double

Cheeseburger
$4.00 Single
$6.50 Double

'Shroom Burger (vegetarian)
$6.50 Crisp-fried portabello filled with melted muenster and cheddar cheese, topped with lettuce, tomato and ShackSauce.

Shack Stack®
$8.50 Cheeseburger and a 'Shroom Burger topped with lettuce, tomato and ShackSauce.

Flat-Top Dogs
Split and griddled crisp.

Shack-cago Dog®
$4.00 Vienna all-beef dog on a potato bun. Dragged through the garden! Topped with Rick's Picks™ Shack relish, onion, cucumber, pickle, tomato, sport pepper, celery salt and mustard.

New York Dog
$3.50 Vienna all-beef dog topped with Schaller & Weber kraut served on a potato bun.

Bird Dog
$4.40 Usinger's Shack chicken sage sausage.

Second City Bird Dog®
$5.40 Bird Dog to Shack-cago clothing, dragged through the garden with Rick's Picks™ Shack Shack relish, onion, cucumber, pickle, tomato, sport pepper, celery salt and mustard.

Fries
100% free of artificial transfats and made from Yukon Gold potatoes. 25% less fat than average fries.

Fries
$3.65

Cheese Fries
$3.65 Topped with our Shack cheddar and American cheese sauce.

Frozen Custard
What happens when soft serve shacks up with premium ice cream!

Shakes
$5.00 Hand-spun vanilla, chocolate, caramel, black & white, strawberry or peanut butter. Make it a malted — add $.50

Fair Shake
$5.80 Vanilla shake spun with 100% certified organic Arabica fairly traded coffee.

Vitamin Creamsicle Shake
$4.75 Vanilla shake blended with David Kirsch Vitamin-Mineral Orange Super Juice

Floats
$4.75 Root beer, purple cow or creamsicle

Cups & Cones
Vanilla, chocolate or flavor of the day
$4.25 Single Dip
$4.35 Double Dip
$5.35 Triple Dip

Sundaes
Add any one topping, whipped cream and a cherry. See below for complete list of toppings & mix-ins
$4.50 Double Dip
$5.50 Triple Dip

Pints To Go
$6.00

Concretes
Dense frozen custard blended at high speed with toppings & mix-ins

The Concrete Jungle
$6.00 Vanilla custard, hot fudge, bananas and peanut butter

Hopscotch
$6.00 Vanilla custard, hot caramel sauce, chocolate toffee and Valrhona chocolate chunks

Shack Attack®
$6.50 Chocolate custard, hot fudge, chocolate truffle cookie dough and Valrhona chocolate chunks, topped with chocolate sprinkles

Concreation Foundation
$4.50 Design your own!

Toppings & Mix-ins
$0.75 each
• hot fudge sauce
• hot caramel sauce
• peanut butter sauce
• chocolate truffle cookie dough
• shortbread cookie
• chocolate toffee • bananas
• whipped cream • salted peanuts
• marshmallow

$1.25 each
• Valrhona chocolate chunks
• seasonal fruit

The Pooch-ini®
$3.75 A chilly treat for those with four feet. ShackBurger dog biscuits, peanut butter sauce and vanilla custard. Includes dairy, sugar and nut products. Not intended for small dogs.

Drinks

Fresh Squeezed Lemonade
$2.40 Regular
$3.05 Large

Fresh Brewed Iced Tea
$1.90 Regular
$2.40 Large

The Arnold Palmer
$1.90 Half lemonade, half iced tea.
$2.40 Regular
Large

Fountain Soda
Coke, Diet Coke, Sprite, Fanta Orange, Fanta Grape, Dr. Pepper
$1.90 Regular
$2.40 Large

Abita Root Beer
$2.65 Abita Brewing Co, Louisiana

Bottled Water
$2.00 Half liter

Beer

Draught
$5.00 ShackMeister® Ale, Brooklyn Brewery, 16oz.

Bottle
$4.50 Budweiser, 16oz.
$4.75 Amstel Light, 12oz.
$5.75 Abita Amber, 12oz.
M.P. Regional Seasonal Bottled Beer

Wine
Check out the menu board for our complete selection.

Stand For Something Good
• We pride ourselves in sourcing premium ingredients. Everything at Shack is made to order.
• Our menu is completely free of artificial trans fats. Ask about our Gluten Free options.
• 100% of our electric usage is offset through Wind Farm credits. We use energy efficient kitchen equipment and compost all of our kitchen food waste.
• We use green materials and sustainable woods in our building designs whenever possible.
* A portion of Shake Shack sales benefit the Madison Square Park Conservancy www.madisonsquarepark.org

Give Some Shack
Gift Cards: Get 'em at the Shack or on our website www.shakeshack.com
Shack Swag: Check out our stock of Shack Gear.

11 Madison AV
NY, NY 10010

SHAKE SHACK

Everyone waiting around you is smiling, a testament to Danny Meyer's creation of a universally appealing fast-food-style burger, the restaurateur equivalent of discovering the golden ratio. Cooks smash freshly ground beef on the griddle until its edges caramelize, top it with American cheese that melts so well it's like an added sauce, and tuck it into a soft potato bun with lettuce, tomato, and Shack Sauce. The somewhat secret blend functions as all traditional condiments — mayo, ketchup, mustard, pickles — in one. There's green scenery and outdoor seating in Madison Square Park, the premier location, not to mention lines. Different outposts offer this bonus: Concretes (really dense shakes) that are inspired by the neighborhood. On the Upper West Side, a Shacky Road spins frozen chocolate custard, chocolate-truffle cookie dough, marshmallow sauce, and almonds.

→ Shake Shack

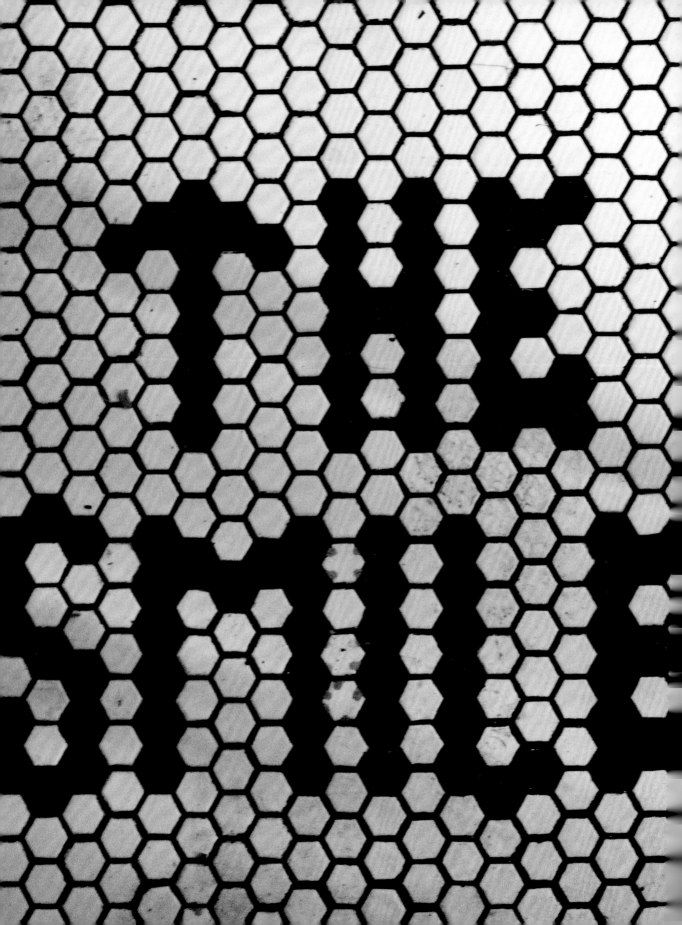

↑ Smile (The)

THE SMILE

Young tastemakers Matt Kliegman and Carlos Quirarte created a fashionable bohemian habitat around simple pleasures: homemade granola, Mariage Frères tea, vegetables sprinkled with olive oil and salt, pretty clientele. Talented curator Luke Scarola, of Brooklyn furniture stop Luddite, designed the space with an 18th-century oil lamp turned chandelier and wood salvaged from Virginia. The partners got the name from a Paris humor journal published in the early 1900s titled *Le Sourire*, and the restaurant's logo features a woman from the 1920s riding a rooster, just because she looks like she's having a good time.

WALK
IN

THE SPOTTED PIG

Lunch

Tuesday, October 4, 2011

Bar Snacks
Roasted Almonds $4
Marinated Olives $4
Pot of Pickles $6
Deviled Egg $4
Chicken Liver Toast $6
Roll Mops $8

Plates
Hurricane Island Oysters with Mignonette 6 for $18 / 12 for $36
Apple Salad with Mrs. Quicke's Cheddar & Walnuts $16
Caesar Salad with Anchovy & Parmesan $15
Pumpkin Salad with San Andreas Cheese & Pinenuts $16
Smoked Haddock Chowder with Homemade Crackers $15
Sheep's Milk Ricotta Gnudi with Brown Butter & Sage $15
Grilled Cheese Sandwich with Onion Marmalade & Mustard $16
Chargrilled Burger with Roquefort & Shoestrings $17
Beer Battered Pollack with Thrice Cooked Chips $17
Cubano Sandwich with Mixed Greens $18

Sides
Shoestring Fries $8
Beets & Greens $8

Desserts
Flourless Chocolate Cake $8
Seasonal Tart $8
Creme Caramel $8
Cheese Plate 2 for $10 / 3 for $15

THE SPOTTED PIG

Hours of Operation

Monday - Friday 12 pm - 2am
Saturday & Sunday 11am - 2am

This is a non-smoking establishment

↑ Spotted Pig (The)

THE SPOTTED PIG

This raucous gastropub owes its success to the inimitable duo of Ken Friedman and chef April Bloomfield. Before putting his convivial talents into restaurants, Friedman earned a reputation for throwing great parties, and Jay-Z is one cool investor-friend who makes regular appearances. Chef April Bloomfield came from London's River Café with a dedication to local ingredients and the novel mission to serve "food that reaches to people's souls: accessible, comforting, and tasty." The simplest market salads are profoundly flavorful, as are savory snacks like chicken-liver toast and pleasingly rich dishes such as sheep's-milk-ricotta gnudi in brown butter. At night, crowds are three rows deep by the bar, and the wait for a table is a few hours. Bloomfield's jovial food includes one of New York's greatest burgers, with its mandatory topping of Roquefort.

314 West 11th ST
NY NY

→ Spotted Pig (The)

URBAN PASTORAL

N° 335

J'AIME NY

72 West 69th ST
NY, NY 10023

→ Telepan

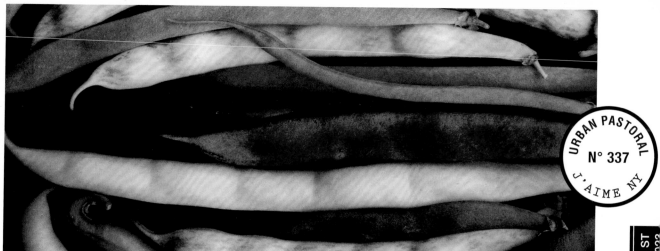

TELEPAN

In August, you're looking at a tomato on your plate and on the wall. Come fall, you'll probably be seeing pears. Blown-up photographs of produce change almost as often as Bill Telepan's New American menu. Diners know Telepan for his house-smoked trout and lobster Bolognese in a light tomato sauce. Local parents are grateful for his work revolutionizing public-school lunches through the Wellness in the Schools program Cook for Kids.

→ Telepan

24 Harrison ST
NY, NY 10009

ARDRAHA

BLU DI BUFALA

BAYLE

→ Terroir

TERROIR

Paul Grieco would like to mold your taste in wine and, most important, get you to drink more Riesling. His manifesto-cum-wine list dedicates 12 pages to the varietal. You'll find German sparklers, bottles from New York's Finger Lakes, and offerings from Hugel in Alsace, Austria's F.X. Pichler, and Selbach-Oster of the Mosel. Other small-production wines fit his qualifications that "the terroir of the grape resonates through the wine." Chef Marco Canora counters his partner's intensity with simple snacks, like lamb sausage wrapped in sage leaves and fried or a melty duck-prosciutto-and-Taleggio sandwich.

→ Torrisi Italian Specialties

TORRISI ITALIAN SPECIALTIES

Chefs Mario Carbone and Rich Torrisi hatched the plan for this neo-Italian-American restaurant as cooks at Café Boulud. Fusing French technique with downtown's immigrant influences, the prix fixe might begin with Cucumbers New Yorkese in various pickled states and end on Island Duck, exotic shorthand for local birds from Long Island. The radical triumph for such a multifarious menu: their devotion to domestic ingredients. Mozzarella is made fresh and served still warm in a bowl of California olive oil; dry pasta hails from Raffetto's, a nearby shop in business since 1906.

250 Mulberry ST
NY, NY 10012

↑ Torrisi Italian Specialties

Union Square
NY, NY 10003

↑ Union Square Greenmarket

KEITHS
ROCAMBOLE
GARLIC
JUMBO SIZE
$1.50 each

UNION SQUARE GREENMARKET

Established in 1976, the city's largest farmers' market connects more than 100 tri-state farmers to tens of thousands of shoppers, four times a week. The presentation is varied and fragrant. In the summer, stands like Berried Treasures lay out extra-sweet Tri-Star strawberries and Sun Gold cherry tomatoes. In the fall and winter, bins overflow with hearty root vegetables that lock in sugars in the cold, and the area's fantastic apples — Macoun, Honey Crisp, and heritage varieties — are for sale by the pound and in the form of hot spiced cider by the cup.

Union Square
NY, NY 10003

↑ Union Square Greenmarket

CAPITAL
TAL
OF THE
WORLD

AREPAS CAFÉ

Venezuelan arepas are delicious stuffed cornmeal patties. The pockets at this familial South American stop in Queens are golden on the outside from the flat-top grill. Roast pork makes an excellent filling with avocado and shredded white cheese. The Arepa Pabellon with shredded beef, black beans, and white cheese also contains fried sweet plantains, which meld seamlessly into the soft steamed interior.

33-07 36th AV
Astoria NY 11106

Bellas Mu...
Picos - Llanos...
Sifrinos - Tierrue...

➤ Arepas Café

BALTHAZAR

TODAY'S SPECIALS

WEDNESDAY
November 6, 2013

DELIVERY

BALTHAZAR
BAKERY
GIFT CARDS
ARE NOW
AVAILABLE
ONLINE!

ONLY ON JUNE

PUMPKIN
CHEESECAKECAKE

SOUP

FRENCH ONION
and
CREAM OF BROCOLI
£7.00

SANDWICH

PASTRAMI PANINO
with sauerkraut, Gruyere and Russian dressing on French rye
$16.75

SALAD

BREADED CHICKEN
with red pepper relish, cherry tomatoes, avocado, buffalo mozzarella,
and house vinaigrette
$16.75

Salads and sandwiches are not available on weekends

Balthazar

BALTHAZAR

Beautifully patinated mirrors reflect towers of fruits de mer zipped through the bustle; brass rails frame burgundy leather banquettes crammed like precious seats on a subway; a golden roast chicken for two, surrounded by browned baby vegetables, lands on the table. Keith McNally conducts this orchestra, a Parisian brasserie through a New York lens. Even sounds resonate, as McNally surely had planned, invigorating the crowd in the room and those sipping good French wine at the bar. The petite bakery next door sells excellent bread, filling sandwiches, and lovely pastries for Francophiles to take away.

BAR

DÉGUSTATION DE LIQUEURS

MARDI

8

NOVEMBRE

CPR KIT
AVAILABLE
TO THE LEFT OF
SERVICE
KITCHEN

Balthazar

198 Grand ST
NY, NY 10013

Saigon

BÁNH MÌ SAIGON

This Vietnamese sandwich shop remains immaculately spare except for a counter selling jewelry by the entrance. No one's buying jade when budget lunch is just a few steps away. In the bánh mì assembly line, a quick prep team stuffs crusty foot-long rolls with sweet pickled carrot shreds and daikon radish, cucumber spears, and a nice selection of fillings. Besides classic options of pork pâté and cold cuts, a filling vegetarian special called the Buddhist has sautéed mushrooms, tofu, and baby corn. Each behemoth comes in a paper pouch. Unwrapping the sandwich bite by bite will save packed toppings from spilling out onto the narrow ledge where customers eat on the spot.

198 Grand ST

→ Bánh Mì Saigon

60 West 55th ST
NY, NY 10019

↑ Benoit

60 West 55th ST
NY, NY 10019

↑ Benoit

BENOIT

Benoit shares its spirit with the Paris original, which was founded in 1912 and has been preserving bistro traditions for 100 years. Chef Philippe Bertineau acts as ambassador in New York, mixing authentic plates like quenelles de brochet and cassoulet with new traditions including the Cookpot, a changing casserole of seasonal vegetables. The bar makes a nice perch for ordering little hors d'oeuvres like cod brandade and a deviled egg mayo — just one if you like. French-pastry lovers always find something to look forward to: the house tart changes every month.

60 West 55th ST
NY, NY 10019

→ Benoit

113 Jane ST
NY, NY 10014

→ Café Gitane

CAFÉ GITANE

The Jane Hotel once sheltered sailors including survivors of the Titanic in 1912. Now stylish and young, it holds this airy French-Moroccan canteen where windows still overlook ships in the Hudson. Waitresses wearing chartreuse shifts deposit smoked-trout salads, molded towers of couscous, and grain toast piled with avocado and chili flakes. As the scene ebbs and flows through all-day service, it changes whether the crowd or staff is more alluring.

→ Café Gitane

CAFÉ GLECHIK

Eastern Europeans still rule Brighton Beach. For Russian food, vodka, and dancing, Tatiana will lure you. For piles of buttery dumplings, there's the Ukrainian Glechik. Two varieties include pelmeni, thin-skinned bundles, and heftier vareniki, with fillings that range from cabbage to veal. Cut the richness the classic way, with BYO vodka.

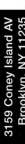

CAPITAL OF THE WORLD
N° 375
J'AIME NY

3159 Coney Island AV
Brooklyn, NY 11235

→ Café Glechik

604 East 187th ST
Bronx, NY 10458

↑ Casa Della Mozzarella

CASA DELLA MOZZARELLA

Off Arthur Avenue — the Little Italy holding on in the Bronx — this old world latticini shop specializes in mozzarella fior di latte (cow's milk) made regularly throughout the day. Varieties come big, small, or as smoked Scamorza balls. One wants to eat such fresh cheeses, so wonderfully pliant and tangy, immediately. Fortunately, the deli counter makes sandwiches on the spot with Italian cold cuts and rolls from Addeo Bakery nearby.

604 East 187th ST
Bronx, NY 10458

→ Casa Della Mozzarella

55 West 35th ST
NY, NY 10001

↑ Cho Dang Gol

CHO DANG GOL

Just off Manhattan's Korea Way — where tabletop grilling joints and karaoke bars run down 32nd Street toward blaring Herald Square — Cho Dang Gol excels in a gentler ceremony. Although those Korean BBQ haunts offer meat with a flash of danger as you drink and duck from flaming coals, here handmade tofu gets its fire from hot chili in traditional stews. The silken soy jiggles apart with the prodding of a spoon in an earthenware bowl.

55 West 35th ST
NY, NY 10001

→ Cho Dang Gol

299 Bowery
NY, NY 10003

→ **DBGB Kitchen & Bar**

DBGB KITCHEN & BAR

"Burgers, bangers, and beer are the mark of the casual me rather than the fancy me uptown. I felt that everywhere you travel in the world, there's always great sausage to discover. We're doing Louisiana andouille with gumbo. Merguez on braised spinach with lemon and mint conveys the rustic and yet exotic flavors of Tunisia. On Sundays, I like the Vermont pork link with oozy Cheddar cheese inside, which is served with a pommes de terre macaire (hash browns), crème fraîche, and a fried egg. The bar focuses on microbreweries; we have 22 beers on draft." —Daniel Boulud

→ DBGB Kitchen & Bar

408 Broome ST
NY, NY 10013

Chupa Chups
$1.00

DESPAÑA

The bull on the wall, known as Pepe, hails from Malaga. Valencia's artisan tiles line the perimeter. You're in the right place for Ibérico ham sliced to order, more than 50 cheeses (from Manchego to Catalonian Garrotxa), and oven-ready churros shipped out of Madrid. Owners Angelica and Marcos Intriago still run the Despaña Brand Foods factory that's produced chorizo in Queens since 1971, but the couple expanded wholesale operations since taking over from the founders. This chic gourmet shop showcases some 400 products imported from Spain. Wonderful things to eat on the premises include tortilla, tapas, and bocadillos (sandwiches) on local ciabatta. The Picante combines house chorizo, Mahon cheese, tomatoes, Basque peppers, and aioli, pressed on the grill. You can order wine here or buy a bottle at their boutique next door.

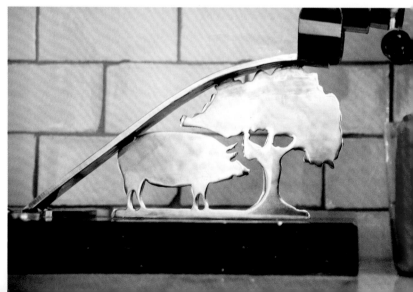

408 Broome ST
NY, NY 10013

➔ Despaña

200 Fifth AV
NY, NY 10010

➜ Eataly

EATALY

Across more than 40,000 square feet, this Italian food emporium mesmerizes with 12 places to eat, including a vegetable antipasti bar, a pizzeria, a meat-focused restaurant called Manzo, and a rooftop beer garden featuring an indie microbrewery. Del Posto's masterminds — Mario Batali, Joe Bastianich, and Lidia Bastianich — partnered with Eataly Turin's founder, Oscar Farinetti, on the astounding project. In between dining stalls, grazers stop for mozzarella made within hours, fresh focaccia, or seafood from the fish counter, among other retail temptations. A produce butcher will even trim your artichokes.

→ Eataly

102 AV C
NY, NY 10009

→ Edi & the Wolf

EDI
& THE WOLF

Some of the fanciful elements that characterize this Austrian wine bar: boots stuffed with flowers, a top-hat lamp, and loops of pirate-worthy rope. Peter Pan would like this place — if he were into Riesling from the Wachau. Chef-partners Eduard "Edi" Frauneder and Wolfgang Ban balance humor with modern plates like cured arctic char and Schlutzkrapfen, Austrian mountain cheese ravioli. There's also an excellent heritage-pork Wiener schnitzel with lingonberry jam.

→ Edi & the Wolf

HANG OVER?
CURE-FOR it!
TRY "UKON"
(TURMERICK) DRINK
SPECIALY formwhay
for hang over
$4.50

MOCHI
ICE CREAMS
BON BON

ESSEX STREET MARKET

Since opening in 1940, this market has hosted
diverse tenants from early Jewish and Italian
vendors to Latin American stalls that now sell
tropical fruits, dried chilies, and bacalao.
The Lower Eastside Girls Club stocks granola and
cookies at La Tiendita as part of a job-training
program. Shopsin's lunch counter carries the
notoriety of curmudgeonly proprietor Kenny
Shopsin and serves hundreds of appetizing
and oddball menu items. Saxelby Cheese has
converted many customers to American cheese.
A highlight of the market, Anne Saxelby's counter
sources the country's best artisanal cheeses
from raw goat's-milk Tomme made in Vermont
by Twig Farm to Ewe's Blue from Old Chatham
Sheepherding Company in New York.

ssex Street Market

120 Essex ST
NY, NY 10002

➤ Essex Street Market, Saxelby Cheesemongers

120 Essex ST
NY, NY 10002

From Evans Farmhouse
NEW yogurt!
MAPLE HILL CREAMERY
Orange VANILLA+ Blueberry
Maple + LEMON + PLAIN
FRESH RICOTTA
QUARK and **FETA**

CHEESE SANDWICHES
ploughman's OR make your own
mini BURRATA
½ OFF! ONLY $2.25
HOT BREAD KI
granola + lav

CHEESE MONGER

Snail of Approval
Slow Food NYC

COLONIE

↑ Essex Street Market, Saxelby Cheesemongers

SAXELBY CHEESEMONGERS

125 West 55th ST
NY NY 10010

→ Estiatorio Milos

ESTIATORIO MILOS

A Greek paean to seafood, Milos presents a study in white. High ceilings and gauzy curtains provide a minimalist backdrop for pristine fish piled on ice in the center of the room like a shrine. It's understood that imports, such as wild loup de mer, need only grilling with some olive oil and lemon. Goat's-milk yogurt makes the best dessert with a twirl of thyme-flower honey from the isle of Kithira.

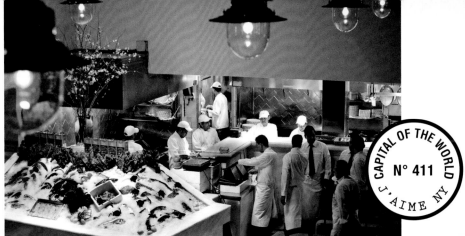

→ Estiatorio Milos

643 Hudson ST
NY NY 10014

→ Fatty Crab

FATTY CRAB

Zak Pelaccio and his affectionately named "Fatty Crew" weave powerful Malaysian flavors into rapid-fire small plates. The loud, lively, and cramped atmosphere of downtown's original Crab echoes the food's intensity. Caramelized pork belly tumbles over cubes of pickled watermelon dressed with lime, ginger, and Thai basil among myriad sweet and sour Southeast Asian ingredients. Having lived in Kuala Lumpur, Pelaccio honors the capital's famous street food in Jalan Alor chicken wings with soy and fish sauces, spices, molasses, and fennel. Signature chili crab takes up an entire bowl like a teenager in a kiddie pool.

643 Hudson ST
NY, NY 10014

→ Fatty Crab

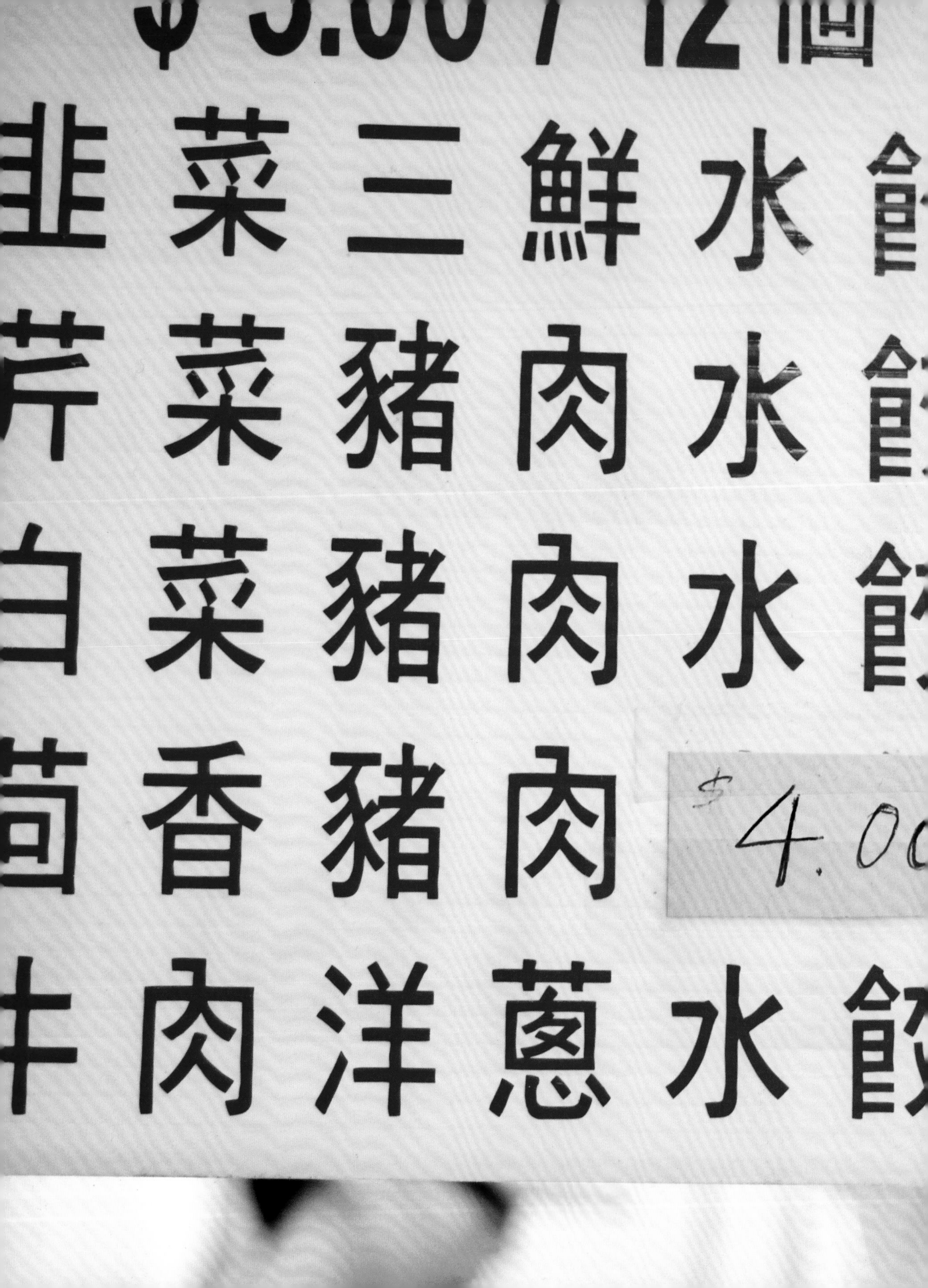

$5.00 / 12個

韭菜三鮮水餃
芹菜豬肉水餃
白菜豬肉水餃
茴香豬肉 $4.00
牛肉洋蔥水餃

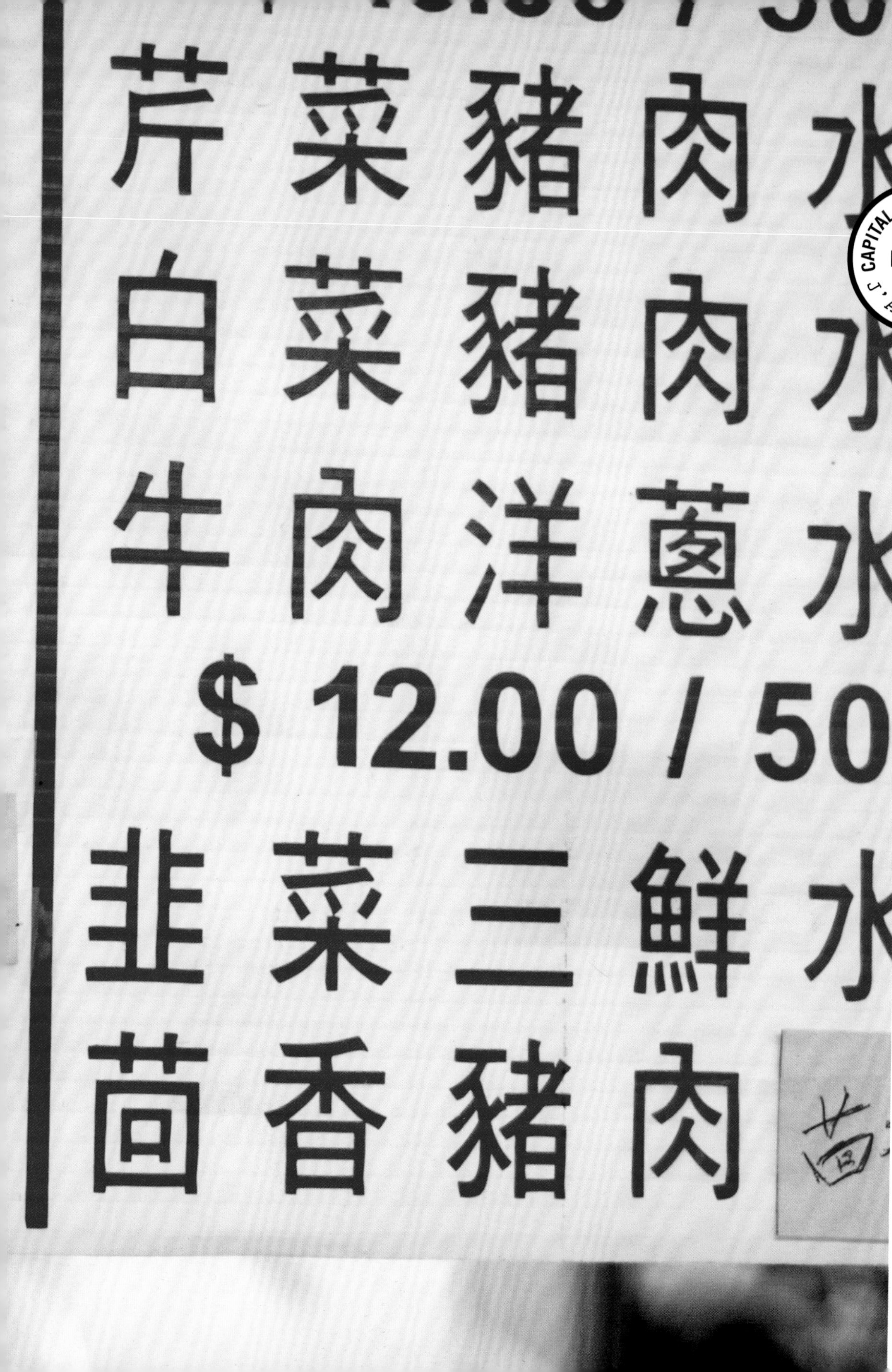
芹菜豬肉水
白菜豬肉水
牛肉洋蔥水
$ 12.00 / 50
韭菜三鮮水
茴香豬肉

CAPITAL OF THE WORLD
N° 417
J'AIME NY

41-28 Main ST
Flushing, NY 11355

→ Golden Mall

油条
肉粥

952
$ 1.00
湯 $ 1.00

EDAY!
$ 5.00
$ 4.50

GOLDEN MALL

There are bountiful things to eat on street level in Flushing's Chinatown — puffy scallion pancakes frying on a griddle, steamed pork buns in baskets — but American banks and pharmacies are still within view. Descend a flight of stairs to Golden Mall's lower level, and you'll be transported to a small maze of regional Chinese vendors. At Xi'an Famous Foods, a woman stretches dough for noodles topped with cumin-fragrant lamb. Across the way at Lanzhou Handmade Noodles, families eat soup at a long table. Xie's Family Dishes sells a dozen juicy dumplings filled with pork, shrimp, and chives for a $3 meal.

蘭州拉麵
Lan Zhou Pulled Noodle

牛肉拉面（刀削面）$5.00
牛雞拉面（刀削面）$6.00
牛尾拉面（刀削面）$6.00
ODLE 牛筋拉面（刀削面）$5.50
牛腩拉面（刀削面）$6.00
海鮮拉面（刀削面）$6.00
蔬菜拉面（刀削面）$4.50
羊肉拉面（刀削面）$6.00
鰻魚拉面（刀削面）$8.50
魚丸拉面（刀削面）$5.00
水餃拉面（刀削面）$5.00

12. WONTON PULLED NOODLE
13. ROAST DUCK PULLED NOODLE
14. STEWED PULLED NOODLE
15. OX TRIPE PULLED NOODLE
16. BEEF INTESTINE PULLED NOODLE
17. PORK INTESTINE PULLED NOODLE
18. TUBE BONE PULLED NOODLE
19. PORK MEAT SAUCE PULLED NOODLE
20. CALM PULLED NOODLE
21. HOUSE SPECIAL HAND PULLED NOODLE
22. HOUSE COLD HAND PULLED NOODLE

刀削麵
SLICED NOODLE

混沌拉面（刀削面）$5.00
烤鴨拉面（刀削面）$5.00
排骨拉面（刀削面）$5.50
牛百葉拉面（刀削面）$5.50
牛壯拉面（刀削面）$5.50
大腸拉面（刀削面）$6.00
筒骨拉面（刀削面）$5.00
炸醬拉面（刀削面）$5.00
海瓜子拉面（刀削面）$6.00
奉揉拉面（刀削面）$6.50
蘭州涼面（刀削面）$3.50

燒
B.

1. SQUID STICK
2. BEEF STICK
3. LAMB STICK
4. CHICKEN ST
5. CHICKEN W
6. CHICKEN
7. FISH BALL
8. MUSHROO
9. TOFU STICK
10. CHICKEN HEAR
11. VEGETABLE STIC

41-28 Main ST
Flushing NY 11355

A2 熱炒涼皮 $5.00
Stir-fried Liang Pi "Cold Skin Noodles"

A3 荞面涼饸饹 $4.50
Buckwheat Cold Noodles

B1 汁肉夹白吉馍 $2.50
Stewed Pork Burger

C1

C2 羊
Lam

C3 羊
Lam

→ Golden Mall

25-12 Steinway ST
Astoria, NY 11103

→ **Kabab Café**

WELCOM
TO
THE
DOMINO
EFFECT

CAPITAL OF THE WORLD
N° 425
J'AIME NY

25-12 Steinway ST
Astoria, NY 11103

→ Kabab Café

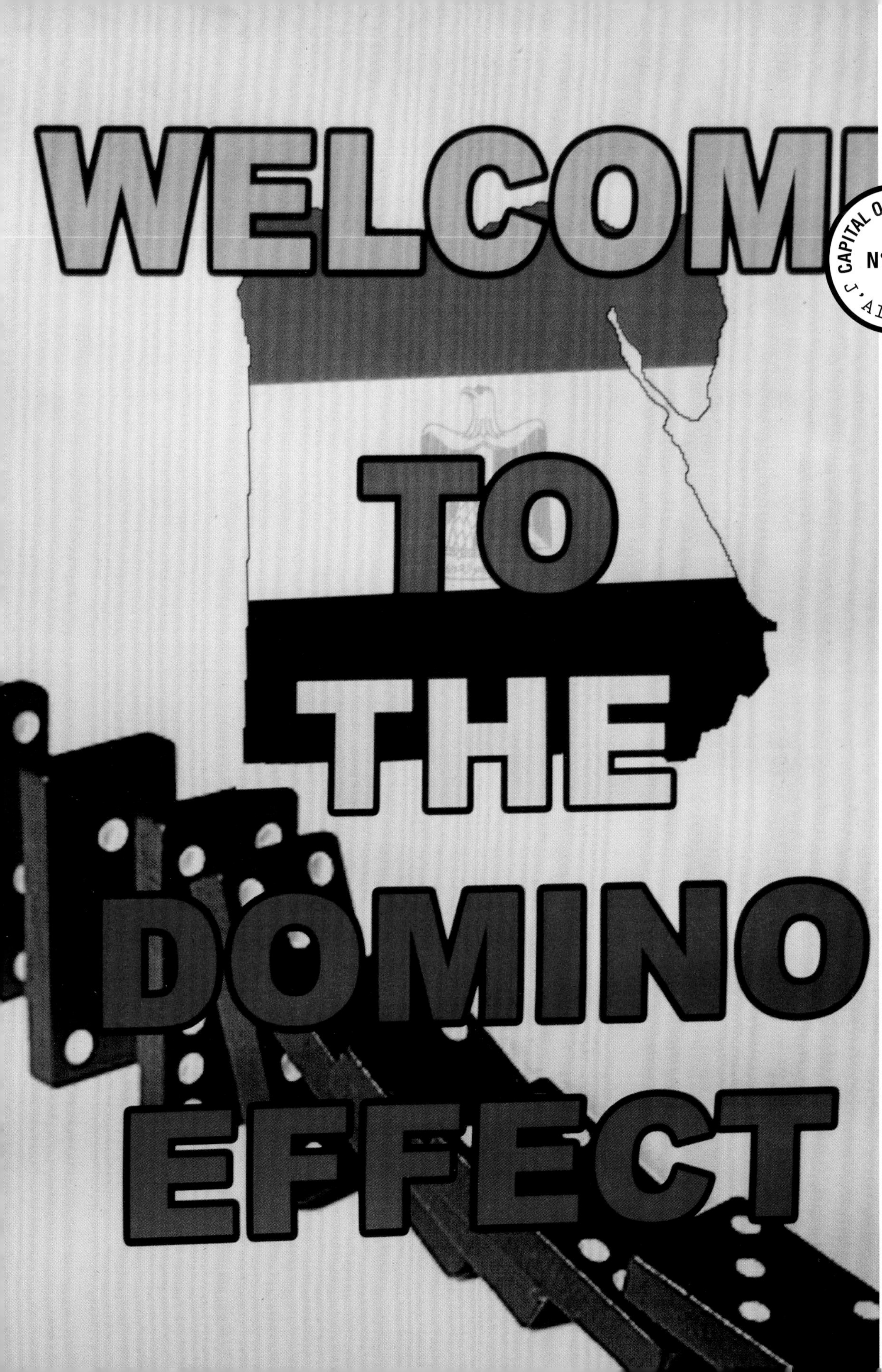

KABAB CAFÉ

Lording over three burners, a convection oven, and some 30 spices, Ali El Sayed channels his birthplace, Alexandria, Egypt. He'll tell you his mother and father were cooks, as was his grandmother; his brother Moustafa runs the larger Mombar just down the block. There are no menus offered. El Sayed starts with the question "Vegetables, meat, or fish?" and discusses what he will make for you. A few clanging pans might yield lamb cheeks simmered in tomato sauce or a vegetarian plate of baba ghanoush with smoked eggplant, hummus, and ovoid falafel perfumed with 18 ingredients from cumin seeds to allspice. The whole plate gets a pouf of sumac and za'atar, a Middle Eastern spice mix that El Sayed calls "the Chanel No. 5 of Egyptian cuisine." Even if you haven't ordered falafel, he might hand one over while you wait.

→ Kabab Café

414 East 9th ST
NY, NY 10003

→ Kajitsu

KAJITSU

The first dish recalls the terrine of autumn vegetables served the previous week but with less green Romanesco and deeper shades of orange squash. The colors transitioned with the progression of fall. Kajitsu's focus is Shojin cuisine, a vegetarian form of Japanese kaiseki first developed by Buddhist monks. In another bowl, matsutake mushroom tempura, resting on soft eggplant, rises out of red miso soup like a flower. These tastes are ephemeral; it's hard to say what will be prepared next month.

→ Kalustyan's

CALIFORNIA
PLUMS
$8.99/LB

IMPORTED/JUMBO
PITTED
PRUNES
$6.99/LB

GLACE
CITRON
HALVES
$14.99/LB

PRUNES
WITH
$4.99

AUSTRALIAN / JUMBO
GLACE
ORANGE
INGREDIENTS: ORANGE, CANE SUGAR, CITRIC ACID, & SODIUM METABISULPHITE.
$12.99/LB

AUSTRALIAN / JUMBO
GLACE
PINEAPPLE
INGREDIENTS: PINEAPPLE, SUGAR, CITRIC ACID, & SODIUM METABISULPHITE.
$12.99/LB

GREE
$6

WE WILL BE
CLOSED
ON THURSDAY
OF NOVEMBER
THANKSGIVING DAY

fresh Herbs
CULINARY

SALAD
GRE

123 Lexington AV
NY NY 10016

KALUSTYAN'S

Created as an Indian specialty food shop in 1944, this compact spice market now proffers thousands of dry goods including seasonings (from Ethiopian berbere to Jordanian za'atar), grains, syrups, and preserved items. An extensive selection of salts ranges from pink Himalayan mountain salt to fleur de sel de Guérande. With every aisle jammed with bits and bobs dedicated to adding flavor to food, Kalustyan's is a sure bet for finding rare ingredients.

→ Kalustyan's

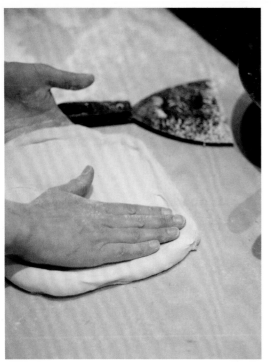

KESTÉ PIZZA & VINO

Pizzaiolo Roberto Caporuscio brings Neapolitan exuberance to this place and its pies. The proud president of the American chapter of the Associazione Pizzaiuoli Napoletani trade association, Caporuscio forms and punches dough, tops it with San Marzano tomatoes and buffalo mozzarella, and fires pizzas quickly in an oven built by experts from Naples. The charred results, with desirable air pockets, prove that perfection often exists on the most elementary level.

271 Bleecker ST

→ Kesté Pizza & Vino

469 Sixth AV
NY, NY 10011

→ Kin Shop

KIN SHOP

After just two revelatory trips to Thailand, New York native Harold Dieterle opened a little Thai restaurant with business partner Alicia Nosenzo. In a casual space with butcher-block tables and teal accents, he elevates Southeast Asian dining. Dieterle blends curry pastes in the open kitchen for dishes like massaman goat neck. He deep-fries oysters for a bright salad with hunks of pork belly and slices crispy-skinned duck breast to wrap in flaky discs of roti. Plating skews Western, as does the headlining dessert: a root-beer float with galangal ice cream.

↑ Kin Shop

114 Kenmare ST
NY, NY 10012

→ La Esquina

MANGO
TORONJA
PIÑA
MANDARINA

AGUAS FRESCAS
JAMAICA
HORCHATA
PIÑA

$2.98

cafe de la

LA ESQUINA

This Soho corner presents Mexican street food three ways. The taqueria counter fires off simple tacos like mahi-mahi with salsa verde. By the hot-sauce table, a bouncer guards a door that claims "Employees Only" but provides access to a sexy, dungeon-like brasserie with an expanded menu. Around the corner, walk-ins go to the casual café. Craft alum Akhtar Nawab's expanded menu downstairs features carnitas tacos with caramelized pork and an earthy purée of huitlacoche, a mushroom-like fungus revered in Mexico. Nawab also runs the Williamsburg location, where dishes might include grilled Mayan prawns in a complex posole-inspired broth. The one constant attraction at all the restaurants: grilled corn covered in mayo and grated cheese.

114 Kenmare ST
NY, NY 10012

La Esquina

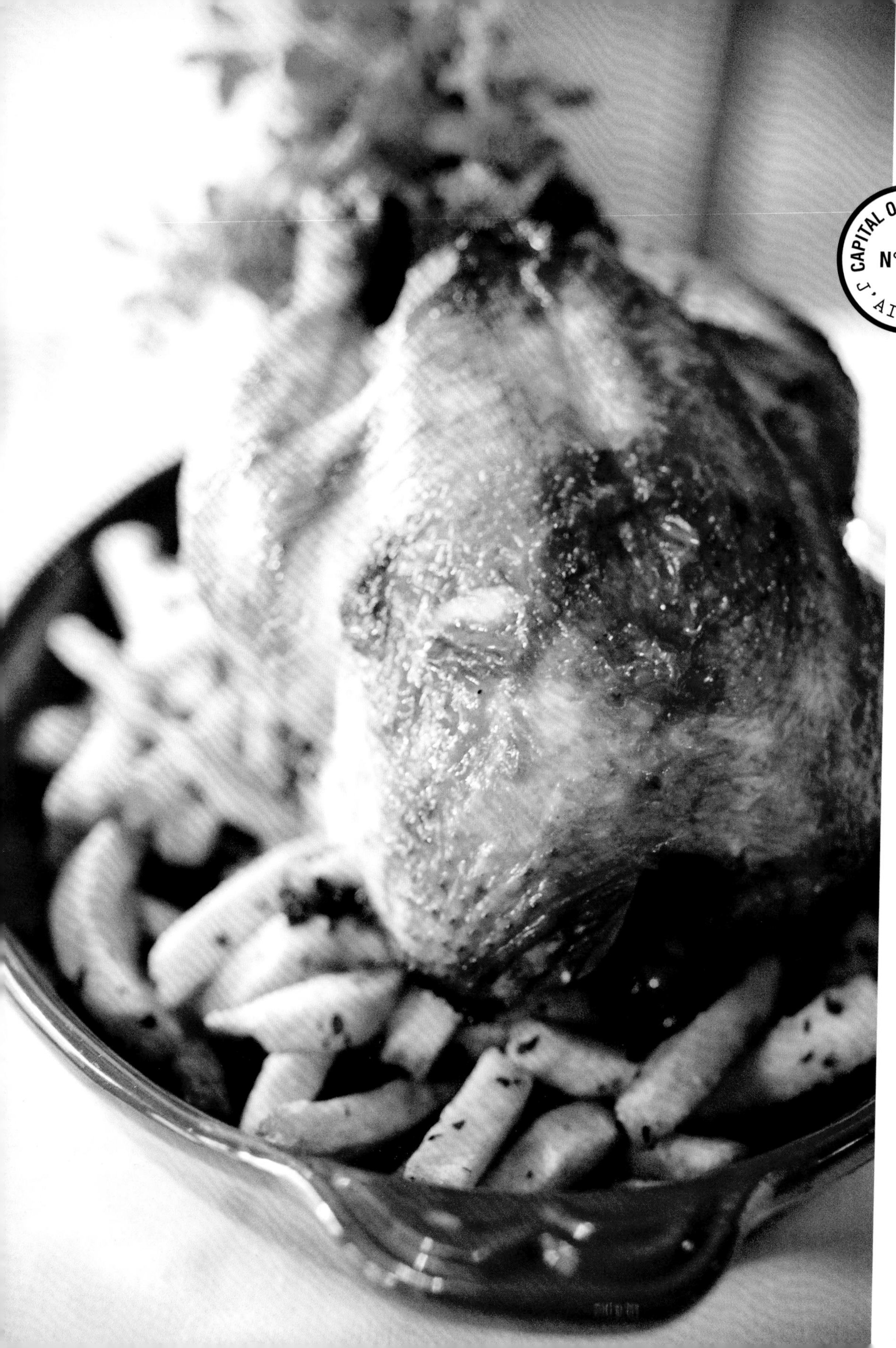

1008 2nd AV
NY, NY 10022

→ La Mangeoire

LA MANGEOIRE

"My mother used to cook for Alain Ducasse when he was a very young chef," remembers owner Gerard Donato, whose father was a maître d' when Ducasse earned two Michelin stars at the Juana Hotel in the south of France. Donato pursued the family métier and opened this neighborhood bistro in 1976. A shift came in 2009 when fine-dining chef Christian Delouvrier decided he wanted to cook country food. Delouvrier delves into heartier dishes like roast chicken over fresh-cut fries, onion soup crowned in Gruyère, and escargot with garlicky tomato confit, Serrano ham, almonds, and mustard. "Sooner or later, you want to do a place like this," says Delouvrier. "We make things we like to eat."

→ La Mangeoire

668 Bay Street
Staten Island, NY 10304

↑ Lakruwana

LAKRUWANA

A ferry ride away from the tip of Manhattan, Staten Island feels more residential and has attracted a wave of immigrants from Sri Lanka, including husband-and-wife restaurateurs Lakruwana and Jayantha Wijesinghe. They've filled the room with traditional masks made to ward off evil, while a small flat-screen above the door broadcasts a tourist-board-like video loop of people riding elephants in the jungle. In the kitchen, Jayantha prepares dishes like hoppers, airy rice-flour pancakes shaped like bowls and served with curry. The house special, lamprais, is a banana-leaf bundle filled with basmati rice, banana curry, toasted cashews, and pieces of hard-cooked egg.

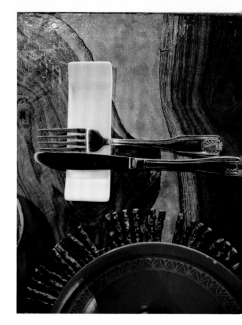

668 Bay Street

→ Lakruwana

37-63 76th ST
Jackson Heights, NY 11372

→ Lali Guras

LALI GURAS

You'll spy fuchsia blossoms on the awning and inside. Lali Gurans are rhododendron, Nepal's national flower. Follow the floral sign to a plastic-coated menu by the register listing "momos." The Himalayan dumplings are stuffed with beef or chicken and fragrant with onion, garlic, and cumin. When Styrofoam plates hit the cramped tables, everyone covers the chewy crimped skins with hot and sesame sauces before spearing away with plastic forks. Vegetarian thalis arrive on round metal trains with little containers of fragrant curry and daal. Though some customers eat with their hands, you won't get odd looks if you use a spoon. If you're lucky, someone will even pop out of the kitchen with rice refills.

764 Amsterdam AV
NY, NY 10025

→ Malecon

MALECON

The Dominican flag might be white, red, and blue, but here la bandera is rice, beans, and rotisserie chicken. Malecon serves Caribbean dishes like mofongo (fried mashed green plantains) and asopado (soupy rice), but glistening birds rotating in the window make a case for ordering a half or quarter of the house specialty. Add some caramelized maduros — sweet plantains — as an extra side.

764 Amsterdam AV

➜ Malecon

304 East 6th ST
NY, NY 10003

→ Mayahuel

MAYAHUEL

In a welcome break from speakeasy-mania, partners Philip Ward, Ravi Derossi, and Justin Shapiro created a temple to tequila and mezcal. Ward's list approaches 70 cocktails like the tart Smoked Palomino with fresh grapefruit, sherry, mescal, and lime. A Suro-Mago combines tequila with elderflower and orange bitters. Named after the Aztec goddess of the maguey plant (a species of agave), the space contains Mexican tiles, stained glass, candles, and enough arches to convey that this place is sacred.

→ Mayahuel

→ Morimoto

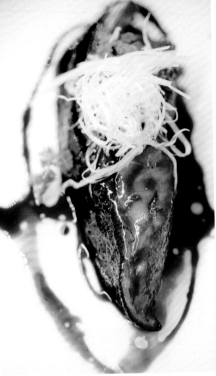

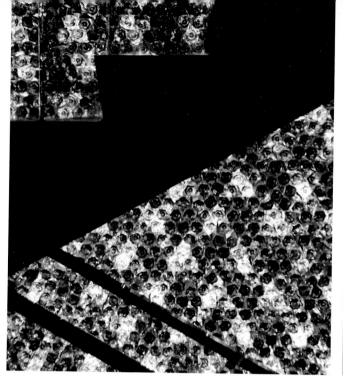

MORIMOTO

Iron Chef Masaharu Morimoto and partner Stephen Starr enlisted one of the most important modern architects in the world, Tadao Ando, to design this 12,000-square-foot space on the western edge of Chelsea Market. Morimoto made just a few requests, including a stage for the sushi bar and limited use of color. Ando answered with an illuminated wooden platform for chefs slicing imported fish and a creamy plaster ceiling that references the sand of a Zen garden and seems to pleat like a curtain. The chef's training may be rooted in Japan, but he embraces outside influences, pairing sashimi with buffalo mozzarella, and roast duck with a foie gras croissant. His restaurants in India influenced the spicy Angry Chicken, flavored with garam masala, cumin, cardamom, and hot sauce.

→ Morimoto

ALL
TRAFFIC

→ N.Y. Dosas

N.Y. DOSAS

There's more to street food than doughy pretzels and chopped-chicken carts. Some famed vendors, like the Arepa Lady, materialize on outer-borough corners, only after certain times at night. Itinerant trucks hawk everything from schnitzel (Schnitzel & Things) to soft-serve ice cream covered in dulce de leche (the Big Gay Ice Cream Truck). Thiru Kumar has sold vegan dosas from this spot for more than a decade, every afternoon but Sunday. New York University students and Greenwich Village regulars stop by for the Pondicherry Masala, a fresh crepe filled with curried potatoes and vegetables. It's no wonder he chose this location: customers can sit down to eat in bustling Washington Square Park.

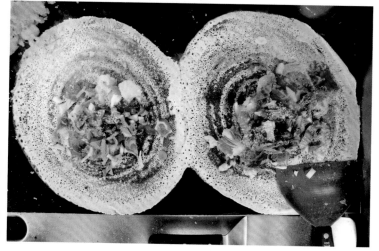

Washington Square Park, South side

N.Y. Dosas

123 Second AV
NY, NY 10003

→ Pommes Frites

ASK FOR FREE SAMPLE!

POMM
Authen

REGULAR	LARGE	DOUBLE
$ 4.50	$ 6.25	$ 7.75

SAUCES : LAYER multiple sauces on frite
EACH side sauce $ 1.00
COMBO of 3 side sauces $ 2.50

ROASTED GARLIC MAYO
ROSEMARY GARLIC MAYO
SWEET MANGO CHUTNEY MAYO
HONEY MUSTARD MAYO
WASABI MAYO
SUNDRIED TOMATO MAYO
HORSERADISH MAYO
PESTO MAYO
DILL LEMON MAYO
SMOKED EGGPLANT MAYO

POMEGRAN
PARMESAN
BLUE CHEE
CHEDDAR
PEANUT SA
MEXICAN
CURRY KET
DIJON MUS
BARBECUE
SWEET CH

FREE : Frite Sauce (traditional european mayo),
Especial (frite sauce, ketchup & onion),
Chopped Raw Onion, Ketchup, Malt Vinegar, Sliced
Tabasco Sauce, Yellow Mustard

Sorry
$50.00

ARGE
6.25

DOUBLE
$ 7.75

REGULAR
$ 4.50

POMMES FRITES

This rustic Belgian-inspired aber-ration pops up on a busy East Vil-lage avenue with an enticing spe-cialization: French fries and a wide variety of fresh sauces. You marvel at the diverse selection while an attendant behind the counter drops rough-cut potatoes into a mix of corn and sunflower oil. The starchy edges fry crisp in varying degrees from soft gold to brown and crunchy. Those who don't take away their paper cones of frites can commandeer a table in the back for easy sit-down dipping. Ketchup, vinegar, and a "European mayo" are free, but it's worth paying $1 for extras like creamy horseradish or sweet-tart pomegranate teriyaki.

→ Pommes Frites

187 Atlantic AV

Brooklyn NY 11201

→ Sahadi's

OSFOR   PAPRIKA   PARSLEY   PEPPER BLACK GROUND   PEPPER BLACK WHOLE

TROPICAL FRUIT MEDLEY
CONTAINS SULFUR
$2.95 LB

SWISS MIX
NO SULFUR
$4.25 LB

DARK CHOCOLATE
MALTED MILK BALLS
$5.50 LB

HOUSE BLEND DECAF
$6.95

ITALIAN DECAF
$8.95 LB

AMERICAN DECAF
$8.95 LB

$8.95

HOUSE BLEND

ITALIAN ROAST

AMERICAN ROAST

FR

SAHADI'S

Sahadi's traces its history back to a Middle Eastern food shop in Manhattan in 1895. Fifty years later, Lebanese founder Wade Sahadi established the current location, and it's still run by the same family. Shoppers come for bulk nuts, dried fruit, and prepared foods like mujadara (lentil-and-rice salad). All sorts of spices include rarities such as Syrian mahlab, derived from the inside of a cherry pit. Olives are also a point of pride: "Lebanese, Moroccan, green, black, wrinkled, and smooth; a big purple one from Chile," lists partner Charlie Sahadi. "People ask, 'Which is the best olive?'" he says. "If there was a best olive, why would I need 36?"

$5.00 Charge for Whining

Whether You Think You Can- Or Think You Can't--You're Probably Right

Did You Ever Stop To Think And Forget To Start Again?

PREMIUM QUALITY AGED RICE

NATURALLY AROMATIC

NET WT. 10 LBS

MOODY

INTERNATIONAL CERTIFICATION ISO 9001:2008 APPROVED

FROM THE FOOTHILLS

→ Sahadi's

211 East 43rd ST

↑ Sakagura

SAKAGURA

Not far from Grand Central Terminal, more than 200 types of sake are tucked away on the lower levels of a midtown office building. At this Japanese drinking den, a sommelier will help pair selections with flavorful snacks: for instance, an omelet with grilled eel and bonito broth, or chilled roasted duck in basil sauce. The most expensive daiginjo styles complement more delicate dishes like fluke sashimi and daikon radish with citrus.

→ Sakagura

306 East 81st ST
NY, NY 10028

→ Sandro's

SANDRO'S

At first look, the space appears plain. Besides sprays of breadsticks, there's little indication of the real vibrant Roman food. Chef Sandro Fioriti, a force of nature, provides the atmosphere. Always there in crazy pants, he bursts in and out of the kitchen at frequent intervals to slice mortadella for familiar faces or even to take orders. In a past life, he says he boxed semi-professionally (under a pseudonym so as to not be discovered by his mother), and it's believable when you see his stature. Fioriti will direct you to his specialties such as crispy fried artichokes splayed out like flowers, bucatini amatriciana, and definitely spaghetti al limone.

306 East 81st ST
NY, NY 10028

Sandro's

30-07 34th ST

→ Seva Indian Cuisine

SEVA INDIAN CUISINE

Immediately, the waiter brings delicate lentil crisps called papadum to shatter and dip into a bright cilantro-mint sauce with notable kick. Tucked into a little café in Astoria, husband-and-wife owners Vinod and chef Charu Sharma make the dishes of Northern India vibrant with details like fresh ginger over creamy chana saag with spinach, tomato, and chickpeas. Tender tandoori chicken tikka is elevated by cucumber raita made in-house.

64-13 39th AV

SRIPRAPHAI

Following turns as a nurse and a baker, Sripraphai Tipmanee opened this restaurant in 1990 to cater to her local Thai community. Considered the place for a Thai-food pilgrimage, the bustling space attracts anyone hunting for pungent tom yum soup filled with oyster mushrooms and drunken noodles sautéed with tomato, basil, and Thai chilies (the idea is that drinking stops the heat). Tossed with shrimp, purple onion, fish sauce, cashews, and more chilies, a unique deep-fried watercress salad has a cult following among chefs. The twinkling summer garden improves an otherwise plain space. As for the name: "We never thought that it would be hard to pronounce because back then 99 percent of our customers were Thai," says Tipmanee's son, Lersak. For the record, it's "see-PRA-pie."

↑ SriPraPhai

347 West 46th ST
NY, NY 10036

Sush of Gari

↑ **Sushi of Gari**

347 West 46th ST
NY NY 10036

SUSHI OF GARI

Masatoshi "Gari" Sugio treats each piece of sushi like a complete dish with seafood, rice, and creative condiments and sauces. He first got the idea while watching diners overuse soy sauce, and this approach leaves seasoning in the hands of the chef. His sushi chefs may top tuna with a creamy tofu purée or add heat to yellowtail with jalapeño sauce, always highlighting the fish.

↑ Sushi of Gari

MAKE YOUR OWN
(CHOOSE TWO FRUITS)
+DATE +PEAR +APPLE
+STRAWBERRY +BANANA
+CANTELOUPE +RASPBERRY
+PINEAPPLE

WHOLE, SKIM OR SOY?
ADD PROTEIN $1.00

BEVERAGES
COKE $2
DIET COKE $2
GINGER ALE $2
SELTZER $2
LIMONATA $2.50
ARANCIATA $2.50

SALADS
PICKLED CABBAGE $4.00
SWEET AND SOUR MARINADE
*GREEK SALAD BOWL $9.50
CHOPPED ROMAINE & ISRAELI SALAD,
KALAMATA OLIVES WITH FETA
TABOULI $5.50
MIXED HERBS, BULGUR WHEAT,
TOMATO, LEMON & OLIVE OIL
ISRAELI $5.00
CHOPPED TOMATO, CUCUMBER, PARSLEY
MOROCCAN CARROTS $5.00
CUMIN, PAPRIKA, GARLIC & OLIVE OIL
MARINATED BEETS $5.00
LEMON, GARLIC, CORIANDER & OLIVE OIL
EGGPLANT SALAD $5.50
SLOW COOKED W/ TOMATO, RED PEPPERS,
ONIONS AND SPICES.

SANDWICHES
FALAFEL $6.25
ONE FLAVOR, WITH HUMMUS,
PICKLED CABBAGE & TAHINI
*SABICH $7.25
FRIED EGGPLANT, ORGANIC EG
ISRAELI SALAD, CABBAGE, TAHIN
HUMMUS $6.00
WITH TAHINI & CHOICE OF TWO

+ASK "WITH EVERYTHING" AN
ADD PICKLES, S'RUG & AMB
+ANY EXTRA SALAD OR SUB B

SAUCES & ADD-ON
(SANDWICHES & PLATTERS)

222 Waverly Place
NY, NY 10014

→ Taïm

222 Waverly PL

TAÏM

Inspired by falafel shops in Tel Aviv, Einat Admony opened this pocket-size storefront with her husband, Stefan Nafziger. The chickpea balls come in three flavors, each fried to order: green herb, spicy harissa, and sweet roasted red pepper. Among the homemade vegetarian spreads and salads, cooks make creamy hummus throughout the day, parsley-bright tabbouleh, and firm, garlicky Moroccan carrots. When you think you've finished the falafel in your warm pita sandwich, you'll happily discover two more hidden under garnishes at the bottom.

→ Taïm

→ Tertulia

TERTULIA

While researching cider houses in Asturias on the northern coast of Spain, Seamus Mullen became fascinated by their aging walls, repaired over time with mixed materials. So he approached this structure like a collage, chipping away brick to make room for wood and stone. The menu also reads like a patchwork. There are tapas and a wood-fired grill to cook everything from paella to a big beautiful steak with browned potatoes. Cheeses and beans may be Asturian, but the framework of each dish is Mullen's obsession with good seasonal products — a consequence of growing up on an organic farm in Vermont.

➜ Tertulia

104-05 47th AV
Corona, NY 11368

→ Tortilleria Nixtamal

TORTILLERIA NIXTAMAL

Corn stalks sometimes sprout from the flower boxes outside this Mexican café and tortilla factory — just one indication that something special can happen in an unexpected place. Inside, owners Fernando Ruiz and Shauna Page practice the widely lost art of nixtamalization, preparing real corn for use in tortillas and tamales. The shop supplies its signature product to well-known Mexican restaurants and serves food. Wrapped in husks like humble presents, tamales release sweet, earthy steam when opened and have generous fillings like poblano chiles and cheese. Tacos come with flavorful meats such as stewed chicken covered in avocado sauce. It's not just nixtamal — everything is made in-house, including chipotle and tomatillo-jalapeño salsas and frothy horchata with cinnamon.

Tortilleria Nixtamal

CAPITAL OF THE WORLD
N° 513
J · AIME NY

366 West 52nd ST
NY, NY 10019

→ Totto Ramen

t table can seat
rties of 4
larger than 4
to be seperated.

Totto Ramen Staff
sorry but...
re not here when
your name, you Must
Bottom of the
Exceptions!!
you for your patience
#Totto Ramen Staff#

TOTTO RAMEN

Elbow to elbow, slurping noodles. This ramen den celebrates its most basic purpose. There's little more on offer than rich chicken-based paitan soup. Have it spicy or not, with a big salty scoop of miso and ground pork or topped with classic char siu pork slices (charred by blowtorch before your eyes). In one distinction from typical ramen joints, seasonal vegetables, avocado, and yuzu paste flavor a vegetarian option: kombu-seaweed-and-shiitake-mushroom soup.

CAPITAL OF THE WORLD

J'AIME NY

N° 517

144 Second AV
NY, NY 10003

→ Veselka

VESELKA & SALMON
EGGS BENEDICT

CHEF'S OMELETTE
SMOKED SALMON,
CREAM CHEESE
& GREEN ONIONS

PIEROGI
(SEASONAL SPECIAL)
SHORT RIB

SPECIAL SOUP
CHRISTMAS BORSCHT
(WITH MUSHROOM DUMPLINGS)

FRESH
APPLE CIDER
SERVED
HOT OR COLD

EGGS BENEDICT
POACHED EGGS &
CANADIAN BACON WITH
HOLLANDAISE SAUCE

GRITS & EGGS
WHITE CORN GRITS WITH
VERMONT CHEDDAR
& POACHED EGGS

GRILLED
MONTE CRISTO
SERVED WITH A
MAPLE MUSTARD SAUCE
& CHOICE OF FRIES

VESELKA
BOWERY
IS NOW OPEN
EAST 1ST & BOWERY

THE BACZYNSKI
(NEW SIGNATURE SANDWICH)
SALAMI, HAM, BACON
PODLASKI
PICKLED VEGETABLES

VESELKA

Downtown's go-to 24-hour diner benefits from atmosphere and borscht (it was founded by a Ukrainian immigrant in 1954 to serve the area's Eastern European population). Now students, old-timers, and late-night oddballs eat cheeseburgers, potato pancakes, sweet blintzes, and pierogies. One of the major differences between Veselka and other diners is that customers return during sober hours to enjoy the same food, along with the spot's enduring energy.

144 Second AV
NY, NY 10003

→ Veselka

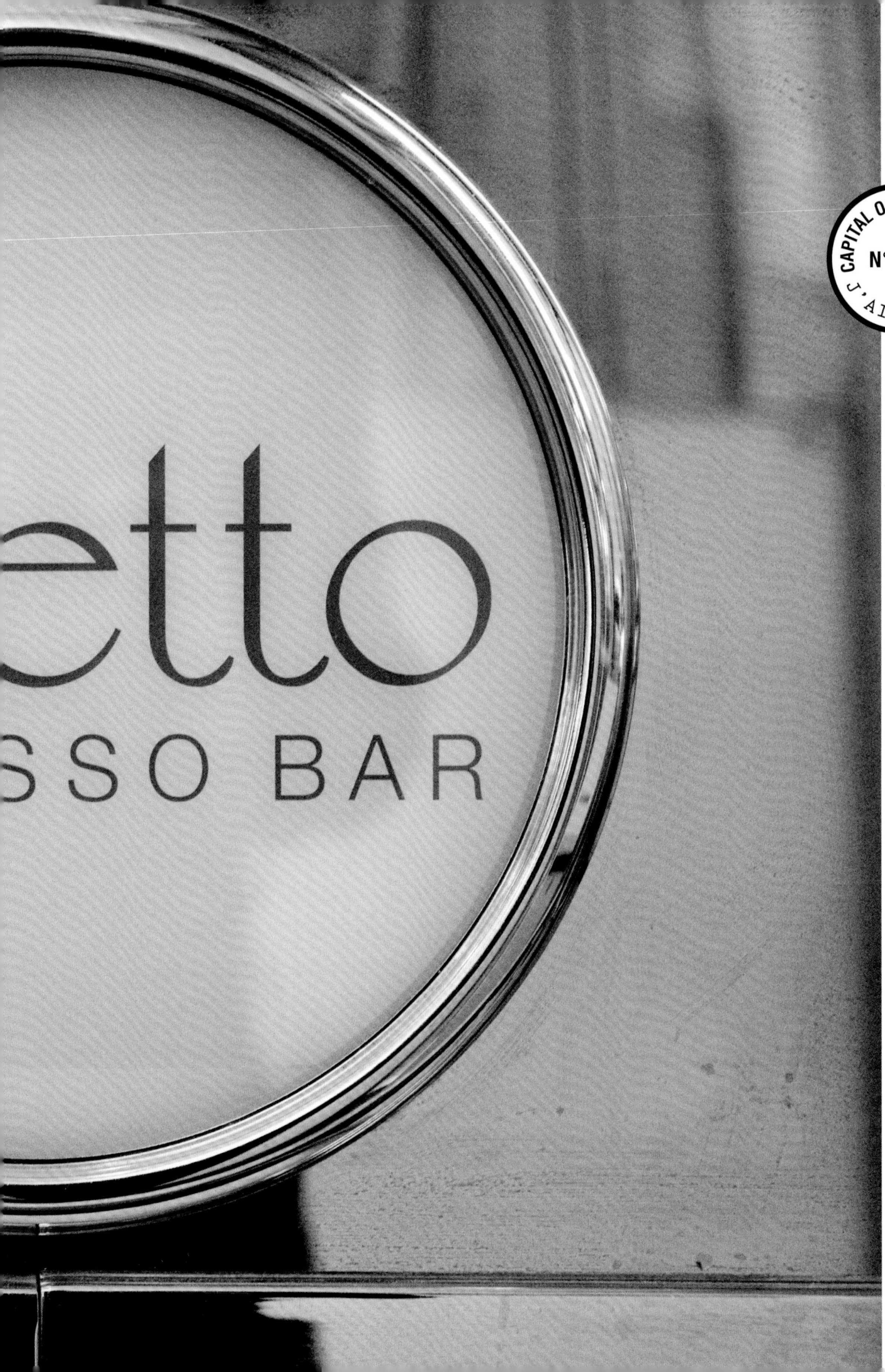

1385 Sixth AV
NY, NY 10019

etto

SSO BAR

→ Zibetto Espresso Bar

ZIBETTO ESPRESSO BAR

If there are others standing over cornetti at the bar, you may have to shuffle into this narrow café sideways. Owner Anastasio Nougos roasts the coffee for espresso in Bologna and imports miniature dunking sweets from Bindi, like tiny chocolate-almond sandwich cookies called baci di dama (lady's kisses). Nougos may run a very Italian operation, but he honed the craft while training as a barista in Sweden.

HOT DRINKS

AFFE	2-3
AFFE AMERICANO	2-3
AFFE MACCHIATO	2.50-3.50
APPUCCINO	3.50
AFFE LATTE	3.50
ECAFFEINATO	2-3
AROCCHINO	3.50
IOCCOLATA CALDA	3.50
EA	2
-SHOT, ICE, SOY	0.50

COLD DRINKS

ICED ITALIAN SPECIAL	3
ICED AMERICANO	2.50
ICED CAPPUCCINO	4
ICED LATTE	4
ICED MAROCCHINO	4
SHEKKERATO	4
AFFOGATO AL CAFFE	3.75
ICED TEA	3
L MONATA-ARANCIATA-CHINOTTO	2.50
COCA COLA	2.50
SUCCHI DI FRUTTA	2
ACQUA MINERALE	2

DESSERTS

ORNETTO	2.50
ILLED CORNETTO	3
IRAMISU	5
ORTA DI FRUTTA	5
OLI	50-4.50
I PAR	4
S	5.50
	0.50

PANINI

TONNO	7.50
CAPRESE	7.50
SOPRESSATA	7.50
PETTO DI POLLO	9
PROSCIUTTO	9
MARINELLA	7.50
TRAMEZZINI	3.25-8.50
PIADINA	8.50

TAX IN

1385 Sixth AV
NY, NY 10019

↑ Zibetto Espresso Bar

SW
EET
LIFE

23-18 31st ST
Astoria, NY 11105

→ Artopolis

ARTOPOLIS

In a mini-mall dedicated to Greek products, Artopolis makes at least 20 varieties of cookies, and small mountains of them are within steps of the door. Recipes come from housewives all over Greece — a project that partner Regina Katopodis says took three years. Kourabiedes threaten to leave powdered-sugar evidence all over your shirt, and storied biscuits include moustokouloura, first flavored with grape-must syrup during wine harvest. Cookies are the initial distraction, but bakers make phyllo dough from scratch for spirals of custard-filled bougasta, pans of dill-and-feta-dappled spinach pie, and various trays of baklava. The honey-covered pastries get that perfect crackle from many coats of clarified imported sheep's butter.

23-18 31st ST

Astoria NY 11105

→ **Artopolis**

BILLY'S BAKERY

The cupcake endures as a pastel anomaly in tough New York City. This simple bomb of butter, flour, and sugar incites a gleeful spectacle wherever it's found. Many purchases take place in 1950s-style bakeries like Billy's, where towering ice-box and coconut cakes are displayed under glass domes. Staffers swirl cream-cheese frosting over red velvet and spiced banana cupcakes. The vanilla buttercream comes in pale shades of pink, yellow, green, or blue because somehow, they say, your favorite color always tastes better.

184 Ninth AV
NY NY 10011

184 9th Ave. · Chelsea · 212.647.9956
75 Franklin St. · Tribeca · 212.647.9958

www.billysbakerynyc.com

Billy's Bakery

160 Prince ST

→ Birdbath

VESUVIO BAKERY

BIRDBATH

The excellent City Bakery's hippie spin-offs run on wind power and receive the flagship's baked goods by bicycle. For the Greenwich Village location, owner Maury Rubin purchased the fabled Vesuvio Bakery space when it closed after 89 years and saved the original storefront. Instead of coal-fired Italian loaves, shoppers stop for squat raspberry bran muffins, signature pretzel croissants, and wholesome lunches like an Old School Veggie Sandwich with sprouts, shredded carrots, and avocado.

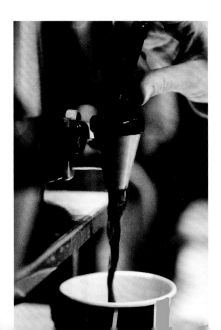

→ Birdbath

513 Henry ST
Brooklyn, NY 11231

Farmacy & Soda Fountain

BROOKLYN FARMACY & SODA FOUNTAIN

"A Pink Poodle and a Purple Cow walk into a bar . . ." That's the beginning (and end) of an ice-cream-float joke told by Peter Freeman, who opened this soda fountain with sister Gia Giasullo. With original pharmaceutical cases and a penny-tile floor, the project harks back to the early 20th century, when drugstores distinguished themselves with sweet, handmade soft drinks. One of Freeman's creations — pink hibiscus syrup with fresh seltzer and Hudson Valley vanilla ice cream — bubbles up like a poodle's pompadour, hence the name. Alongside staple egg creams and sundaes, seasonal syrups invigorate the menu so the Purple Cow made with Concord grape soda is available only through fall. The siblings have preserved a piece of culinary history, and their old-fashioned utopia is further defined by its clientele: "On any given day you can have age ranges from 6 to 80 all at the same counter. There are people born and raised here and people who came here a month ago, and everybody is finding something in this place, something here that they love," says Freeman.

513 Henry ST
Brooklyn, NY 11231

→ Brooklyn Farmacy & Soda Fountain

SWEET LIFE

N° 543

J'AIME NY

1048 Fifth AV
NY, NY 10028

→ Café Sabarsky

CAFÉ SABARSKY

In addition to Austro-German art, the mansion turned Neue Galerie houses the city's best strudel. Below Gustav Klimt's golden Adele Bloch-Bauer and decorative Bauhaus pieces, chef Kurt Gutenbrunner's café transports you to a turn-of-the-century Viennese setting identified by marble tables, silver trays carrying dark roast coffee, and sconces designed by celebrated artist Josef Hoffmann. It's lovely here in streaming sunlight. The classic apple pastry is on tantalizing display with other desserts, like a house Klimt-tort combining thin layers of hazelnut cake and a cloak of dark-chocolate ganache.

➜ Café Sabarsky

75 Ninth AV

→ Chelsea Market

CHELSEA MARKET

- BUDDAKAN
- BUON' ITALIA
- CHELSEA MARKET BASKETS
- CHELSEA NEWS
- CHELSEA THAI
- CHELSEA WINE VAULT
- THE CLEAVER COMPANY
- DICKSON'S FARMSTAND MEATS
- ELENI'S NEW YORK
- FAT WITCH BAKERY
- THE FILLING STATION
- FRIEDMAN'S LUNCH
- GRAMERCY PARK FLOWER SHOP
- THE GREEN TABLE
- HALE AND HEARTY
- IMPORTS FROM MARRAKESH
- JACQUES TORRES CHOCOLATE
- L'ARTE DEL GELATO
- THE LOBSTER PLACE
- LUCY'S WHEY
- MANHATTAN FRUIT EXCHANGE
- MORIMOTO
- NINTH STREET ESPRESSO
- THE NUT BOX SPICES
- PEOPLE'S POPS
- POSMAN BOOKS
- RONNYBROOK MILK BAR
- RUTHY'S BAKERY & CAFE
- SARABETH'S BAKERY

CHELSEA MARKET

Cookies have come out of this complex since the 1890s, when the National Biscuit Company (later known as Nabisco) produced crackers and, by 1912, those famous Oreos. Old factory floors and exposed brick hint at the past, but independent bakeries like Sarabeth's, with her artisanal fruit jams, and Amy's Bread now occupy the space. It's not all sweet these days. Buon Italia sells fresh and dry pasta, semolina flour, and burrata. Ronnybrook Milk Bar serves eggs and sandwiches in addition to shakes. Dickson's stocks farm-raised meats, there's a fish market, and Bowery Kitchen Supply equips chefs and civilians with knives and last-minute cooking tools.

SWEET LIFE
N° 549
J'AIME NY

75 Ninth AV
NY, NY 10011

→ Chelsea Market

PAIN A...
CHOCOLA...
$3.25

...COOKIES
$2.50

75 Ninth AV
NY, NY 10011

→ Chelsea Market, Amy's Bread

AMY'S BREAD

↑ Chelsea Market, Buon Italia

PORCHETTA
ALLA ROMANA
HOMEMADE
$ 16.95/LB.

PANCETTA

COPPA
SWEET & HOT

PERONI ARROSTITI

MARINATED ROASTED PEPPERS

buon Italia

→ Chelsea Market, Buon Italia

BUON ITALIA

DESSERT CLUB CHIKALICIOUS

Japanese pastry chef Chika Tillman and husband Don run this sweets counter as a playful annex to their dainty dessert bar across the street. Tillman's luscious vanilla-bean soft-serve stars in a sundae covered with chocolate pearls, shredded phyllo dough, and salted pistachios. Cupcakes benefit from skillful restraint: flavors like red velvet, double chocolate, and salted caramel come with just a dollop of silky buttercream.

➜ Dessert Club Chikalicious

220 West 23rd ST
NY, NY 10011

← Doughnut Plant

DOUGHNUT PLANT

A doughnut innovator, Mark Israel makes seasonal fruit glazes, fills Blackout cake with chocolate cream, and trademarked the Jelly Filled Square (house-made jam in every bite). His doughnut ballooned with crème brûlée might be the most popular order, but the Chelsea location sells an oatmeal cake ring — sprinkled with oats and bits of dried fruit — that's a textural masterpiece. If you can take your eyes away from what's left in the case, you'll see doughnut shapes everywhere from the tiles on the wall to the backs of wooden chairs.

SWEET LIFE
N° 561
J'AIME NY

220 West 23rd ST
NY, NY 10011

➜ Doughnut Plant

SWEET LIFE

N° 563

J'AIME NY

108 Rivington ST
NY, NY 10002

→ Economy Candy

ECONOMY CANDY

What began as a typical penny candy shop in 1937 now provides a snapshot of America's confectionary history. Nostalgia seekers find retro Mallo Cups and milk-chocolate Sky Bars known for compartmentalized fillings of caramel, vanilla, peanut, and fudge. Bins hold gummies, bulk gumballs, and M&M's, divided so that you can actually hoard different colors.

→ Economy Candy

439 Third AV
Brooklyn, NY 11215

➜ Four & Twenty Blackbirds

FOUR & TWENTY BLACKBIRDS

"This must be where pies go when they die" reads a sign by the door. That's an inviting message for homemade-pie lovers looking to take down a slice. Sisters Melissa and Emily Elsen learned about ample all-butter crusts from their grandmother, who developed her own following as a pie baker in South Dakota. In an old-fashioned way, neighbors settle in over pastries and coffee. The Elsens experiment with seasonal fillings, balancing sweetness with savory elements as in bourbon pear or salty honey custard for fall and strawberry balsamic or wild ginger apricot in summer.

PIE by the SL[ICE]

APPLE .75
EGG IN A NEST 4.50/5.50 WITH BACON
GRANOLA w/ MILK 4
      w/ YOGURT 4.50
BAG O' GRANOLA 9
      1 POUND
HOT CHOCOLATE 2.50/3.50
HOUSE SODA 2
COLD BREW ICED COFFEE 3
ICED MINT TEA 2.50
CIDER SPRITZER 2.50
HOT CIDER 2.50

Salty Honey
Bittersweet Chocolate
Maple Buttermilk Custard
Salted Caramel Apple

439 Third AV
Brooklyn, NY 11215

CASH ONLY!

→ Four & Twenty Blackbirds

SWEET LIFE
N° 571
J'AIME NY

116 West Houston ST
NY, NY 10012

116 WEST HOUSTON STREET NY

→ FPB Bakery

FPB BAKERY

Before launching this café and bakery, François Payard made pastries for French restaurants from La Tour d'Argent in Paris to Daniel in New York. Now, you can watch how he makes macarons in the glass-framed sweets factory. Attempting to overrule the cupcake, at least in Soho, he creates wild macaron flavors like cookies 'n cream or seasonal pumpkin. Payard also sneaks in very traditional pastries such as a gâteau Basque with fragrant almond cake and sturdy vanilla pastry cream.

116 West Houston ST
NY NY 10012

↑ FPB Bakery

82 Berry ST
Brooklyn, NY 10003

↑ Hotel Delmano

HOTEL DELMANO

Temptation appears in many forms. At this bar, no one seems to realize that the city is a place where you should constantly be in a rush. A ceiling fan ticks slowly; drinkers lean back at café tables and pluck oysters from frosty pedestals; the bartender takes his time making your drink. A romantic design warrants the lingering, as do cocktails like the Devil's Garden: reposado tequila, sweet agave, bitter Cynar, and mint with the gradual heat of chipotle-infused mezcal.

→ Hotel Delmano

ON / PREPARAZIONE

KITCHEN, A TRAINED AND ATTENTIVE STAFF TRANSFORMS
TED RAW INGREDIENTS. WE JUICE AND ZEST LEMONS,
D PEACHES, PIT CHERRIES, PLUMS AND MANGOES,
PEARS AND PINEAPPLES. INFUSION IS ANOTHER
SS. TO EXTRACT FLAVOR, WE STEEP COFFEES AND TEAS
S INTO OUR BASE, AND THEN STRAIN. ADDITIONALLY,
PISTACHIOS AND ALMONDS, PICK AND STEM HERBS
AND LAVENDER, AND, OF COURSE, WE SEED VANILLA
OUR OWN EXTRACTS. AND SO MUCH MORE.

SWEET LIFE
N° 579
J'AIME NY

188 Ludlow ST
NY NY 10002

↑ Il Laboratorio del Gelato

IL LABORATORIO
DEL GELATO

There are multiple expressions of different fruits and chocolates at this gelati and sorbetti shop, which speaks to the purity of each flavor. Five kinds of fig gelato spotlight fresh and dry varieties, and sorbets like grapefruit (with or without Campari) are so true to taste that it's as though there's no need for sugar. Founder Jon F. Snyder's futuristic lab spans nearly 3,000 square feet, and you can watch the pristine production of some 200 flavors through a glass partition. In the case up front, nearly 50 selections ranging from acacia honey to yuzu change daily, so it can take time deliberating on what to commit to in a cup.

→ Il Laboratorio del Gelato

"Bakers Of The World's Finest Carrot Cake."

www.lloydscarrotcake.com

"Made From Scratch."

Lloyd's

CARROT CAKE

(kd)

→ **Lloyd's Carrot Cake**

LLOYD'S CARROT CAKE

The cake here stays so moist that presliced wedges retain an impeccably tender crumb. Your most important decision is ordering with or without raisins and walnuts; otherwise, both versions of carrot cake have the same spiced batter and thick cream-cheese frosting. Garnet red velvet, chocolate, and nicely spongy coconut slices round out the time-honored layer-cake offerings.

6087 Broadway
Bronx, NY 10471

→ Lloyd's Carrot Cake

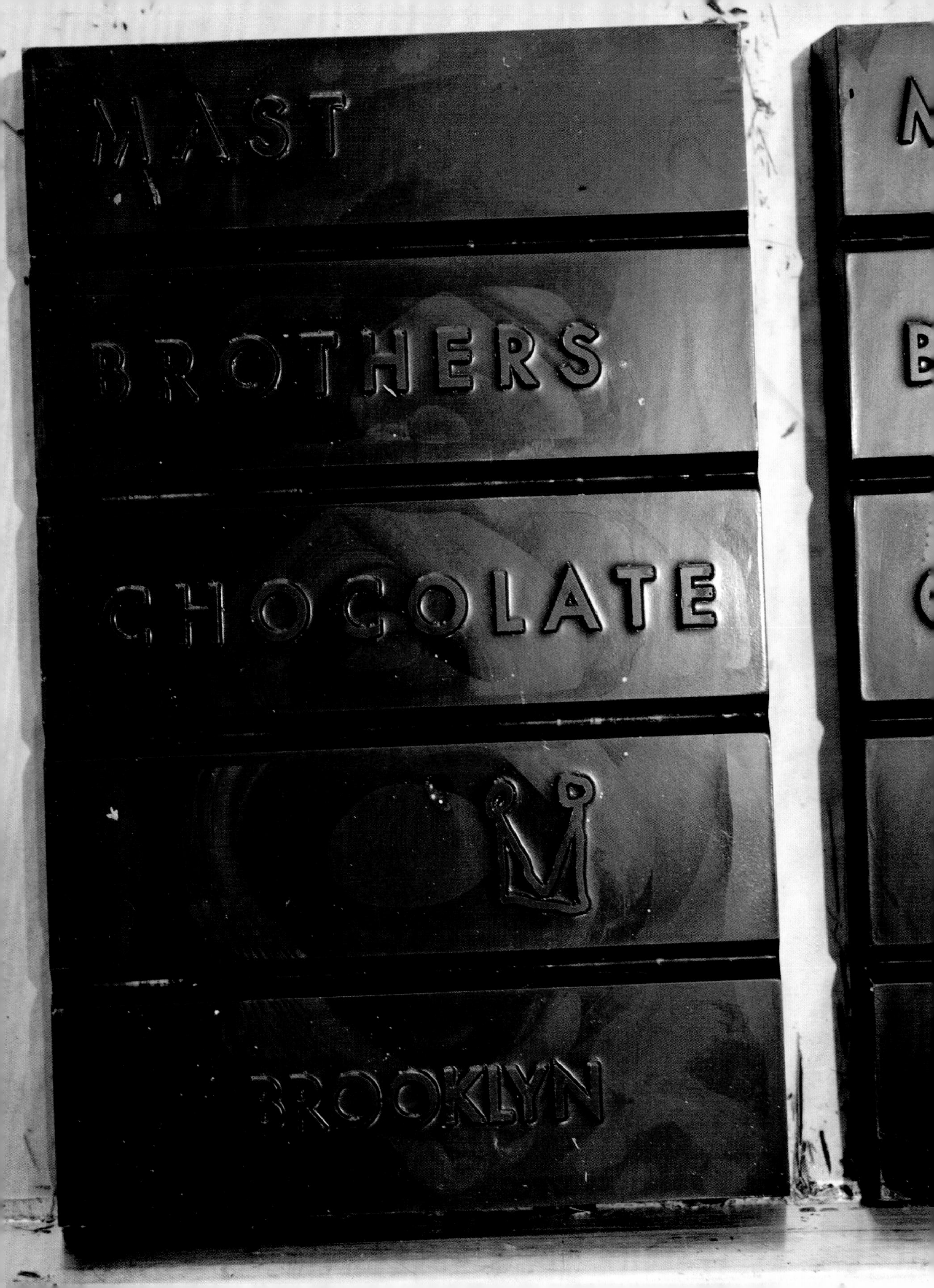
MAST
BROTHERS
CHOCOLATE
BROOKLYN

111 North 3rd ST
Brooklyn, NY 11211

→ Mast Brothers Chocolate

111 North 3rd ST
Brooklyn, NY 11211

MAST BROTHERS CHOCOLATE

Brothers Rick and Michael Mast launched a bean-to-bar chocolate operation in Brooklyn, producing bars with ingredients as simple as cacao and cane sugar. Highlighting the distinctive flavors of organic, direct-trade beans, the Masts use minimal additions like crunchy cocoa nibs, almonds with salt, or serrano pepper; many other selections are single-origin. Their artisanship extends to wrappers that recall the quality of Florentine paper but feature custom patterns such as anchors, cocoa pods, and high-wheel bicycles. Since the factory expanded by 3,000 square feet and added a test kitchen, pastries are another reason to visit the Brooklyn tasting room.

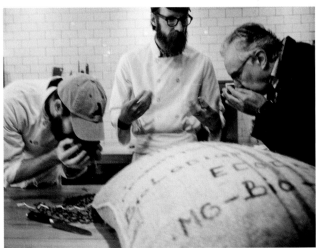

→ Mast Brothers Chocolate

68 Dean ST
Brooklyn, NY 11201

↑ One Girl Cookies

ONE GIRL COOKIES

The stylish approach to tea cookies comes from owner Dawn Casale, who left a career at Barneys department store to bake. Each piece in her collection warrants close attention. The Penelope, based on an aunt's recipe for buttery apricot thumbprints, is coated with roasted, chopped almonds and walnuts. Whoopie pies — little chocolate or pumpkin cake sandwiches filled with cream-cheese frosting — are too tempting to admire for long.

↑ One Girl Cookies

533 West 47th ST
NY, NY 10036

→ Sullivan Street Bakery

SULLIVAN STREET BAKERY

As shocking as this may be, New York's bread maestro doesn't hail from France. Jim Lahey built his reputation by re-creating Italian peasant breads he tasted while traveling through Tuscany. Lahey's top loaves feature rough well-done crusts that shatter at the outer shell and give way to sourdough interiors. Ultra-thin Roman-style pizzas favor minimal toppings like a glaze of tomato or shaved potatoes, which curl and crisp under high heat. Sandwiches also stay focused, usually with three key ingredients like mortadella, fontal cheese, and olive salad.

Biscotti Pratessi
with almond
$8.00

SULLIVAN ST
BAKERY

→ Sullivan Street Bakery

81 Bergen ST
Brooklyn, NY 11217

→ Van Leeuwen Artisan Ice Cream

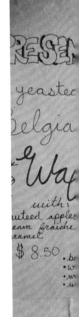

organic.

les!
plain - $6

try a waffle
Sundae!

$9.50

VAN LEEUWEN ARTISAN ICE CREAM

Starting with just a 1988 Chevy Step Van painted butter yellow and plans to serve good ice cream from a truck, brothers Ben and Peter Van Leeuwen, with Ben's wife, Laura O'Neill, went on to launch a fleet of Mr. Softee competitors and multiple stores. The young entrepreneurs also designed this location. A friend created the wallpaper based on botanical drawings for different ingredients like Tahitian vanilla orchids, Hudson Valley red currants, and Sicilian pistachios. Each flavor's creaminess comes from 18 percent butter, achieved with egg yolks and milk from Battenkill Valley upstate.

↑ Van Leeuwen Artisan Ice Cream

ALPHABETICAL INDEX

BOOK	GUIDE			
21	4	'21' Club	RESTAURANT	Midtown West

A

BOOK	GUIDE			
173	16	ABC Kitchen	RESTAURANT	Flatiron District
177	16	Abraço Espresso	COFFEE SHOP	East Village
180	16	Ace Hotel	HOTEL	Flatiron District
180	16	Ace Hotel: Breslin (The)	RESTAURANT	Flatiron District
180	16	Ace Hotel: John Dory Oyster Bar (The)	RESTAURANT	Flatiron District
191	17	Aldea	RESTAURANT	Flatiron District
26	4	Annisa	RESTAURANT	West Village
193	17	Ardesia	RESTAURANT	Hell's kitchen
354	32	Arepas Café	RESTAURANT	Astoria
528	46	Artopolis	BAKERY	Astoria

B

BOOK	GUIDE			
28	4	Bagel Hole	BAKERY	Park Slope
358	32	Balthazar	RESTAURANT, BAKERY	Soho
362	32	Bánh Mì Saigon	RESTAURANT	Little Italy
196	17	Bedford Cheese Shop	CHEESE SHOP	Williamsburg
368	33	Benoit	RESTAURANT	Midtown West
533	46	Billy's Bakery	BAKERY	Chelsea
537	46	Birdbath	BAKERY	Soho
201	18	Blue Hill at Stone Barns	RESTAURANT	Pocantico Hills
33	5	Blue Ribbon	RESTAURANT	Soho
204	18	Booker and Dax	BAR	East Village
36	5	Bouley	RESTAURANT	Tribeca
209	18	Broadway Panhandler	KITCHEN STORE	Greenwich Village
212	18	Brooklyn Brewery	BREWERY	Williamsburg
540	47	Brooklyn Farmacy & Soda Fountain	ICE CREAM SHOP	Carroll Gardens
217	19	Brooklyn Flea/Smorgasburg	MARKET	Williamsburg
40	5	Burger Joint	RESTAURANT	Midtown West

C

BOOK	GUIDE			
372	33	Café Gitane	RESTAURANT	West Village
374	33	Café Glechik	RESTAURANT	Brighton Beach
545	47	Café Sabarsky	RESTAURANT	Upper West Side
378	33	Casa Della Mozzarella	CHEESE SHOP	The Bronx
42	5	Chef's Table at Brooklyn Fare	RESTAURANT	Downtown Brooklyn
549	47	Chelsea Market: Amy's Bread	BAKERY	Chelsea
555	47	Chelsea Market: Buon Italia	GOURMET SHOP	Chelsea
382	34	Cho Dang Gol	RESTAURANT	Midtown East
219	19	Ciano	RESTAURANT	Flatiron District
45	6	Corton	RESTAURANT	Tribeca
222	19	Craft	RESTAURANT	Flatiron District
225	20	Crush Wine & Spirits	WINE MERCHANT	Midtown East

D

BOOK	GUIDE			
228	20	Daisy May's BBQ USA	RESTAURANT	Hell's kitchen
50	6	Daniel	RESTAURANT	Upper West Side

387	34	DBGB Kitchen & Bar	RESTAURANT	East Village
54	6	Del Posto	RESTAURANT	Chelsea
232	20	Dell' anima	RESTAURANT	West Village
390	34	Despaña	GOURMET SHOP	Soho
557	48	Dessert Club Chikalicious	BAKERY	East Village
237	21	Diner	RESTAURANT	Williamsburg
561	48	Doughnut Plant	BAKERY	Chelsea
241	21	Dovetail	RESTAURANT	Upper West Side

E

395	35	Eataly	MARKET	Flatiron District
565	48	Economy Candy	CANDY SHOP	Lower East Side
398	35	Edi & the Wolf	RESTAURANT	East Village
402	35	Essex Street Market, Saxelby Cheesemongers	CHEESE SHOP	Lower East Side
410	36	Estiatorio Milos	RESTAURANT	Midtown West

F

59	6	Fairway	SUPERMARKET	Upper West Side
414	36	Fatty Crab	RESTAURANT	West Village
245	21	Fette Sau	RESTAURANT	Williamsburg
568	48	Four & Twenty Blackbirds	BAKERY	Gowanus
62	7	Four Seasons Restaurant (The)	RESTAURANT	Midtown East
573	49	FPB BAKERY	BAKERY	Soho
248	22	Franny's	RESTAURANT	Park Slope

G

418	36	Golden Mall	FOOD COURT	Flushing
253	22	Good Fork (The)	RESTAURANT	Red Hook
66	7	Gotham Bar and Grill	RESTAURANT	Greenwich Village
71	7	Gramercy Tavern	RESTAURANT	Flatiron District

H

| 576 | 49 | Hotel Delmano | BAR | Williamsburg |

I

| 580 | 49 | Il Laboratorio del Gelato | ICE CREAM SHOP | Lower East Side |

J

75	7	J.G. Melon	BAR	Upper West Side
79	8	Jean Georges	RESTAURANT	Upper West Side
257	22	Joseph Leonard	RESTAURANT	West Village

K

426	37	Kabab Café	RESTAURANT	Astoria
431	37	Kajitsu	RESTAURANT	East Village
435	37	Kalustyan's	GOURMET SHOP	Murray Hill
82	8	Katz's Delicatessen	RESTAURANT	Lower East Side
86	8	Keens	RESTAURANT	Midtown West
436	38	Kesté Pizza & Vino	RESTAURANT	Greenwich Village

ALPHABETICAL INDEX

BOOK	GUIDE			
441	38	Kin Shop	RESTAURANT	West Village
89	8	King Cole Bar	BAR	Midtown East
259	23	Kitchen Arts & Letters	BOOKSTORE	Upper West Side

L

BOOK	GUIDE			
445	38	La Esquina	RESTAURANT	Soho
91	9	La Grenouille	RESTAURANT	Midtown East
448	38	La Mangeoire	RESTAURANT	Midtown East
452	39	Lakruwana	RESTAURANT	Staten Island
457	39	Lali Guras	RESTAURANT	Jackson Heights
95	9	Le Bernardin	RESTAURANT	Midtown West
99	9	Le Cirque	RESTAURANT	Midtown East
262	23	Little Owl (The)	RESTAURANT	West Village
584	50	Lloyd's Carrot Cake	BAKERY	The Bronx
103	9	Locanda Verde	RESTAURANT	Tribeca
266	23	Luke's Lobster	RESTAURANT	East Village

M

BOOK	GUIDE			
460	39	Malecon	RESTAURANT	Upper West Side
107	10	Marea	RESTAURANT	Upper West Side
589	50	Mast Brothers Chocolate	CHOCOLATE SHOP	Williamsburg
464	39	Mayahuel	BAR	East Village
271	23	Mile End	RESTAURANT	Boerum Hill
110	10	Minetta Tavern	RESTAURANT	Greenwich Village
275	24	Momofuku Ssäm Bar	RESTAURANT	East Village
114	10	Monkey Bar	RESTAURANT	Midtown East
469	40	Morimoto	RESTAURANT	Chelsea
278	24	Motorino	RESTAURANT	East Village

N

BOOK	GUIDE			
472	40	N.Y. Dosas	FOOD CART	Greenwich Village
118	11	Nobu	RESTAURANT	Tribeca

O

BOOK	GUIDE			
282	24	O. Ottomanelli & Sons	BUTCHER	West Village
593	51	One Girl Cookies	BAKERY	Cobble Hill

P

BOOK	GUIDE			
286	25	Peasant	RESTAURANT	Nolita
291	25	Peels	RESTAURANT	East Village
123	11	Peter Luger	RESTAURANT	Williamsburg
295	25	Pies 'n' Thighs	RESTAURANT	Williamsburg
126	11	Plaza Food Hall by Todd English (The)	FOOD COURT	Midtown East
477	40	Pommes Frites	RESTAURANT	East Village
298	26	Porchetta	RESTAURANT	East Village
303	26	Prime Meats	RESTAURANT	Carroll Gardens
305	26	Prune	RESTAURANT	East Village

BOOK	GUIDE			
		R		
130	11	Red Cat (The)	RESTAURANT	Chelsea
309	26	Red Farm	RESTAURANT	West Village
135	12	Red Rooster	RESTAURANT	Harlem
312	27	Roberta's	RESTAURANT	Bushwick
316	27	Russ & Daughters	GOURMET SHOP	Lower East Side
		S		
481	41	Sahadi's	GOURMET SHOP	Cobble Hill
485	41	Sakagura	BAR	Midtown East
321	27	Saltie	RESTAURANT	Williamsburg
489	41	Sandro's	RESTAURANT	Upper West Side
493	41	Seva Indian Cuisine	RESTAURANT	Astoria
325	28	Shake Shack	RESTAURANT	Flatiron District
329	28	Smile (The)	RESTAURANT	Noho
332	28	Spotted Pig (The)	RESTAURANT	West Village
495	42	SriPraPhai	RESTAURANT	Woodside
141	12	Standard (The)	HOTEL, RESTAURANT	Meatpacking District
596	51	Sullivan Street Bakery	BAKERY	Hell's Kitchen
499	42	Sushi of Gari	RESTAURANT	Midtown West
		T		
503	42	Taïm	RESTAURANT	West Village
337	29	Telepan	RESTAURANT	Upper West Side
341	29	Terroir	BAR	Tribeca
507	42	Tertulia	RESTAURANT	West Village
145	12	Time Warner Center: A Voce	RESTAURANT	Upper West Side
147	12	Time Warner Center: Bouchon Bakery	BAKERY	Upper West Side
151	12	Time Warner Center: Masa	RESTAURANT	Upper West Side
156	13	Time Warner Center: Per Se	RESTAURANT	Upper West Side
158	13	Time Warner Center: Porter House New York	RESTAURANT	Upper West Side
344	29	Torrisi Italian Specialties	RESTAURANT	Nolita
511	43	Tortilleria Nixtamal	RESTAURANT	Corona
162	13	Totonno's Pizzeria Napolitano	RESTAURANT	Coney Island
515	43	Totto Ramen	RESTAURANT	Hell's Kitchen
		U		
349	29	Union Square Greenmarket	MARKET	Union Square
		V		
601	51	Van Leeuwen Artisan Ice Cream	ICE CREAM SHOP	Boerum Hill
519	43	Veselka	RESTAURANT	East Village
		W		
167	13	wd~50	RESTAURANT	Lower East Side
		Z		
522	43	Zibetto Espresso Bar	COFFEE SHOP	Midtown West

INDEX BY LOCATION

BOOK GUIDE

THE BRONX

Belmont
378 33 Casa Della Mozzarella CHEESE SHOP

Riverdale
584 50 Lloyd's Carrot Cake BAKERY

BROOKLYN

Boerum Hill
271 23 Mile End RESTAURANT
601 51 Van Leeuwen Artisan Ice Cream ICE CREAM SHOP

Brighton Beach
374 33 Café Glechik RESTAURANT

Bushwick
312 27 Roberta's RESTAURANT

Carroll Gardens
540 47 Brooklyn Farmacy & Soda Fountain ICE CREAM SHOP
303 26 Prime Meats RESTAURANT

Cobble Hill
593 51 One Girl Cookies BAKERY
481 41 Sahadi's GOURMET SHOP

Coney Island
162 13 Totonno's Pizzeria Napolitano RESTAURANT

Downtown Brooklyn
42 5 Chef's Table at Brooklyn Fare RESTAURANT

Gowanus
568 48 Four & Twenty Blackbirds BAKERY

Park Slope
28 4 Bagel Hole BAKERY
248 22 Franny's RESTAURANT

Red Hook
253 22 Good Fork (The) RESTAURANT

Williamsburg
196 17 Bedford Cheese Shop CHEESE SHOP
212 18 Brooklyn Brewery BREWERY
217 19 Brooklyn Flea/Smorgasburg MARKET
237 21 Diner RESTAURANT
245 21 Fette Sau RESTAURANT
576 49 Hotel Delmano BAR
589 50 Mast Brothers Chocolate CHOCOLATE SHOP
123 11 Peter Luger RESTAURANT
295 25 Pies 'n' Thighs RESTAURANT
321 27 Saltie RESTAURANT

MANHATTAN

Chelsea
533 46 Billy's Bakery BAKERY
549 47 Chelsea Market: Amy's Bread BAKERY
555 47 Chelsea Market: Buon Italia GOURMET SHOP
54 6 Del Posto RESTAURANT
561 48 Doughnut Plant BAKERY

BOOK	GUIDE		
469	40	Morimoto	RESTAURANT
130	11	Red Cat (The)	RESTAURANT

East Village

177	16	Abraço Espresso	COFFEE SHOP
204	18	Booker and Dax	BAR
387	34	DBGB Kitchen & Bar	RESTAURANT
557	48	Dessert Club Chikalicious	BAKERY
398	35	Edi & the Wolf	RESTAURANT
431	37	Kajitsu	RESTAURANT
266	23	Luke's Lobster	RESTAURANT
464	39	Mayahuel	BAR
275	24	Momofuku Ssäm Bar	RESTAURANT
278	24	Motorino	RESTAURANT
291	25	Peels	RESTAURANT
477	40	Pommes Frites	RESTAURANT
298	26	Porchetta	RESTAURANT
305	26	Prune	RESTAURANT
519	43	Veselka	RESTAURANT

Flatiron District

173	16	ABC Kitchen	RESTAURANT
180	16	Ace Hotel	HOTEL
180	16	Ace Hotel: Breslin (The)	RESTAURANT
180	16	Ace Hotel: John Dory Oyster Bar (The)	RESTAURANT
191	17	Aldea	RESTAURANT
219	19	Ciano	RESTAURANT
222	19	Craft	RESTAURANT
395	35	Eataly	MARKET
71	7	Gramercy Tavern	RESTAURANT
325	28	Shake Shack	RESTAURANT

Greenwich Village

209	18	Broadway Panhandler	KITCHEN STORE
66	7	Gotham Bar and Grill	RESTAURANT
436	38	Kesté Pizza & Vino	RESTAURANT
110	10	Minetta Tavern	RESTAURANT
472	40	N.Y. Dosas	FOOD CART

Harlem

| 135 | 12 | Red Rooster | RESTAURANT |

Hell's Kitchen

193	17	Ardesia	RESTAURANT
228	20	Daisy May's BBQ USA	RESTAURANT
596	51	Sullivan Street Bakery	BAKERY
515	43	Totto Ramen	RESTAURANT

Little Italy

| 362 | 32 | Bánh Mì Saigon | RESTAURANT |

Lower East Side

565	48	Economy Candy	CANDY SHOP
402	35	Essex Street Market, Saxelby Cheesemongers	CHEESE SHOP
580	49	Il Laboratorio del Gelato	ICE CREAM SHOP
82	8	Katz's Delicatessen	RESTAURANT
316	27	Russ & Daughters	GOURMET SHOP
167	13	wd~50	RESTAURANT

Meatpacking District

| 141 | 12 | Standard (The) | HOTEL, RESTAURANT |

INDEX BY LOCATION

BOOK	GUIDE		
		Midtown East	
382	34	Cho Dang Gol	RESTAURANT
225	20	Crush Wine & Spirits	WINE MERCHANT
62	7	Four Seasons Restaurant (The)	RESTAURANT
89	8	King Cole Bar	BAR
91	9	La Grenouille	RESTAURANT
448	38	La Mangeoire	RESTAURANT
99	9	Le Cirque	RESTAURANT
114	10	Monkey Bar	RESTAURANT
126	11	Plaza Food Hall by Todd English (The)	FOOD COURT
485	41	Sakagura	BAR
		Midtown West	
21	4	'21' Club	RESTAURANT
368	33	Benoit	RESTAURANT
40	5	Burger Joint	RESTAURANT
410	36	Estiatorio Milos	RESTAURANT
86	8	Keens	RESTAURANT
95	9	Le Bernardin	RESTAURANT
499	42	Sushi of Gari	RESTAURANT
522	43	Zibetto Espresso Bar	COFFEE SHOP
		Murray Hill	
435	37	Kalustyan's	GOURMET SHOP
		Noho	
329	28	Smile (The)	RESTAURANT
		Nolita	
286	25	Peasant	RESTAURANT
344	29	Torrisi Italian Specialties	RESTAURANT
		Soho	
358	32	Balthazar	RESTAURANT, BAKERY
537	46	Birdbath	BAKERY
33	5	Blue Ribbon	RESTAURANT
390	34	Despaña	GOURMET SHOP
573	49	FPB Bakery	BAKERY
445	38	La Esquina	RESTAURANT
		Tribeca	
36	5	Bouley	RESTAURANT
45	6	Corton	RESTAURANT
103	9	Locanda Verde	RESTAURANT
118	11	Nobu	RESTAURANT
341	29	Terroir	BAR
		Union Square	
349	29	Union Square Greenmarket	MARKET
		Upper West Side	
545	47	Café Sabarsky	RESTAURANT
50	6	Daniel	RESTAURANT
241	21	Dovetail	RESTAURANT
59	6	Fairway	SUPERMARKET
75	7	J.G. Melon	BAR
79	8	Jean Georges	RESTAURANT
259	23	Kitchen Arts & Letters	BOOKSTORE
460	39	Malecon	RESTAURANT
107	10	Marea	RESTAURANT
489	41	Sandro's	RESTAURANT
337	29	Telepan	RESTAURANT

145	12	Time Warner Center: A Voce	RESTAURANT
147	12	Time Warner Center: Bouchon Bakery	BAKERY
151	12	Time Warner Center: Masa	RESTAURANT
156	13	Time Warner Center: Per Se	RESTAURANT
158	13	Time Warner Center: Porter House New York	RESTAURANT

West Village

26	4	Annisa	RESTAURANT
372	33	Café Gitane	RESTAURANT
232	20	Dell' anima	RESTAURANT
414	36	Fatty Crab	RESTAURANT
257	22	Joseph Leonard	RESTAURANT
441	38	Kin Shop	RESTAURANT
262	23	Little Owl (The)	RESTAURANT
282	24	O. Ottomanelli & Sons	BUTCHER
309	26	Red Farm	RESTAURANT
332	28	Spotted Pig (The)	RESTAURANT
503	42	Taïm	RESTAURANT
507	42	Tertulia	RESTAURANT

QUEENS

Astoria

354	32	Arepas Café	RESTAURANT
528	46	Artopolis	BAKERY
426	37	Kabab Café	RESTAURANT
493	41	Seva Indian Cuisine	RESTAURANT

Corona

| 511 | 43 | Tortilleria Nixtamal | RESTAURANT |

Flushing

| 418 | 36 | Golden Mall | FOOD COURT |

Jackson Heights

| 457 | 39 | Lali Guras | RESTAURANT |

Woodside

| 495 | 42 | SriPraPhai | RESTAURANT |

STATEN ISLAND

Staten Island

| 452 | 39 | Lakruwana | RESTAURANT |

WESTCHESTER

Tarrytown

| 201 | 18 | Blue Hill at Stone Barns | RESTAURANT |

INDEX BY CATEGORY

BOOK	GUIDE		
		BAKERY	
528	46	Artopolis	ASTORIA
28	4	Bagel Hole	PARK SLOPE
358	32	Balthazar Bakery	SOHO
533	46	Billy's Bakery	CHELSEA
537	46	Birdbath	SOHO
549	47	Chelsea Market: Amy's Bread	CHELSEA
557	48	Dessert Club Chikalicious	EAST VILLAGE
561	48	Doughnut Plant	CHELSEA
568	48	Four & Twenty Blackbirds	GOWANUS
573	49	FPB Bakery	SOHO
584	50	Lloyd's Carrot Cake	THE BRONX
593	51	One Girl Cookies	COBBLE HILL
596	51	Sullivan Street Bakery	HELL'S KITCHEN
147	12	Time Warner Center: Bouchon Bakery	UPPER WEST SIDE
		BAR	
204	18	Booker and Dax	EAST VILLAGE
576	49	Hotel Delmano	WILLIAMSBURG
75	7	J.G. Melon	UPPER WEST SIDE
89	8	King Cole Bar	MIDTOWN EAST
464	39	Mayahuel	EAST VILLAGE
485	41	Sakagura	MIDTOWN EAST
341	29	Terroir	TRIBECA
		BOOKSTORE	
259	23	Kitchen Arts & Letters	UPPER WEST SIDE
		BREWERY	
212	18	Brooklyn Brewery	WILLIAMSBURG
		BUTCHER	
282	24	O. Ottomanelli & Sons	WEST VILLAGE
		CANDY SHOP	
565	48	Economy Candy	LOWER EAST SIDE
		CHEESE SHOP	
196	17	Bedford Cheese Shop	WILLIAMSBURG
378	33	Casa Della Mozzarella	THE BRONX
402	35	Essex Street Market, Saxelby Cheesemongers	LOWER EAST SIDE
		CHOCOLATE SHOP	
589	50	Mast Brothers Chocolate	WILLIAMSBURG
		COFFEE SHOP	
177	16	Abraço Espresso	EAST VILLAGE
522	43	Zibetto Espresso Bar	MIDTOWN WEST
		FOOD CART	
472	40	N.Y. Dosas	GREENWICH VILLAGE

FOOD COURT

| 418 | 36 | Golden Mall | FLUSHING |
| 126 | 11 | Plaza Food Hall by Todd English (The) | MIDTOWN EAST |

GOURMET SHOP

555	47	Chelsea Market: Buon Italia	CHELSEA
390	34	Despaña	SOHO
435	37	Kalustyan's	MURRAY HILL
316	27	Russ & Daughters	LOWER EAST SIDE
481	41	Sahadi's	COBBLE HILL

HOTEL

| 180 | 16 | Ace Hotel | FLATIRON DISTRICT |
| 141 | 12 | Standard (The) | MEATPACKING DISTRICT |

HOTEL, RESTAURANT

| 141 | 12 | Standard Grill (The) | MEATPACKING DISTRICT |

ICE CREAM SHOP

540	47	Brooklyn Farmacy & Soda Fountain	CARROLL GARDENS
580	49	Il Laboratorio del Gelato	LOWER EAST SIDE
601	51	Van Leeuwen Artisan Ice Cream	BOERUM HILL

KITCHEN STORE

| 209 | 18 | Broadway Panhandler | GREENWICH VILLAGE |

MARKET

217	19	Brooklyn Flea/Smorgasburg	WILLIAMSBURG
395	35	Eataly	FLATIRON DISTRICT
349	29	Union Square Greenmarket	UNION SQUARE

RESTAURANT

21	4	'21' Club	MIDTOWN WEST
173	16	ABC Kitchen	FLATIRON DISTRICT
180	16	Ace Hotel: Breslin (The)	FLATIRON DISTRICT
180	16	Ace Hotel: John Dory Oyster Bar (The)	FLATIRON DISTRICT
191	17	Aldea	FLATIRON DISTRICT
26	4	Annisa	WEST VILLAGE
193	17	Ardesia	HELL'S KITCHEN
354	32	Arepas Café	ASTORIA
358	32	Balthazar	SOHO
362	32	Bánh Mì Saigon	LITTLE ITALY
368	33	Benoit	MIDTOWN WEST
201	18	Blue Hill at Stone Barns	POCANTICO HILLS
33	5	Blue Ribbon	SOHO
36	5	Bouley	TRIBECA
40	5	Burger Joint	MIDTOWN WEST
372	33	Café Gitane	WEST VILLAGE
374	33	Café Glechik	BRIGHTON BEACH
545	47	Café Sabarsky	UPPER WEST SIDE

INDEX BY CATEGORY

BOOK	GUIDE		
42	5	Chef's Table at Brooklyn Fare	DOWNTOWN BROOKLYN
382	34	Cho Dang Gol	MIDTOWN EAST
219	19	Ciano	FLATIRON DISTRICT
45	6	Corton	TRIBECA
222	19	Craft	FLATIRON DISTRICT
228	20	Daisy May's BBQ USA	HELL'S KITCHEN
50	6	Daniel	UPPER WEST SIDE
387	34	DBGB Kitchen & Bar	EAST VILLAGE
54	6	Del Posto	CHELSEA
232	20	Dell' anima	WEST VILLAGE
237	21	Diner	WILLIAMSBURG
241	21	Dovetail	UPPER WEST SIDE
398	35	Edi & the Wolf	EAST VILLAGE
410	36	Estiatorio Milos	MIDTOWN WEST
414	36	Fatty Crab	WEST VILLAGE
245	21	Fette Sau	WILLIAMSBURG
62	7	Four Seasons Restaurant (The)	MIDTOWN EAST
248	22	Franny's	PARK SLOPE
253	22	Good Fork (The)	RED HOOK
66	7	Gotham Bar and Grill	GREENWICH VILLAGE
71	7	Gramercy Tavern	FLATIRON DISTRICT
79	8	Jean Georges	UPPER WEST SIDE
257	22	Joseph Leonard	WEST VILLAGE
426	37	Kabab Café	ASTORIA
431	37	Kajitsu	EAST VILLAGE
82	8	Katz's Delicatessen	LOWER EAST SIDE
86	8	Keens	MIDTOWN WEST
436	38	Kesté Pizza & Vino	GREENWICH VILLAGE
441	38	Kin Shop	WEST VILLAGE
445	38	La Esquina	SOHO
91	9	La Grenouille	MIDTOWN EAST
452	39	Lakruwana	STATEN ISLAND
457	39	Lali Guras	JACKSON HEIGHTS
448	38	La Mangeoire	MIDTOWN EAST
95	9	Le Bernardin	MIDTOWN WEST
99	9	Le Cirque	MIDTOWN EAST
262	23	Little Owl (The)	WEST VILLAGE
103	9	Locanda Verde	TRIBECA
266	23	Luke's Lobster	EAST VILLAGE
460	39	Malecon	UPPER WEST SIDE
107	10	Marea	UPPER WEST SIDE
271	23	Mile End	BOERUM HILL
110	10	Minetta Tavern	GREENWICH VILLAGE
275	24	Momofuku Ssäm Bar	EAST VILLAGE
114	10	Monkey Bar	MIDTOWN EAST
469	40	Morimoto	CHELSEA
278	24	Motorino	EAST VILLAGE
118	11	Nobu	TRIBECA
286	25	Peasant	NOLITA

291	25	Peels	EAST VILLAGE
123	11	Peter Luger	WILLIAMSBURG
295	25	Pies 'n' Thighs	WILLIAMSBURG
477	40	Pommes Frites	EAST VILLAGE
298	26	Porchetta	EAST VILLAGE
303	26	Prime Meats	CARROLL GARDENS
305	26	Prune	EAST VILLAGE
130	11	Red Cat (The)	CHELSEA
309	26	Red Farm	WEST VILLAGE
135	12	Red Rooster	HARLEM
312	27	Roberta's	BUSHWICK
321	27	Saltie	WILLIAMSBURG
489	41	Sandro's	UPPER WEST SIDE
493	41	Seva Indian Cuisine	ASTORIA
325	28	Shake Shack	FLATIRON DISTRICT
329	28	Smile (The)	NOHO
332	28	Spotted Pig (The)	WEST VILLAGE
495	42	SriPraPhai	WOODSIDE
499	42	Sushi of Gari	MIDTOWN WEST
503	42	Taïm	WEST VILLAGE
337	29	Telepan	UPPER WEST SIDE
507	42	Tertulia	WEST VILLAGE
145	12	Time Warner Center: A Voce	UPPER WEST SIDE
151	12	Time Warner Center: Masa	UPPER WEST SIDE
156	13	Time Warner Center: Per Se	UPPER WEST SIDE
158	13	Time Warner Center: Porter House New York	UPPER WEST SIDE
344	29	Torrisi Italian Specialties	NOLITA
511	43	Tortilleria Nixtamal	CORONA
162	13	Totonno's Pizzeria Napolitano	CONEY ISLAND
515	43	Totto Ramen	HELL'S KITCHEN
519	43	Veselka	EAST VILLAGE
167	13	wd~50	LOWER EAST SIDE

SUPERMARKET

| 59 | 6 | Fairway | UPPER WEST SIDE |

WINE MERCHANT

| 225 | 20 | Crush Wine & Spirits | MIDTOWN EAST |

ACKNOWLEDGEMENTS

J'aime New York.
I feel happy here, at peace with myself and with others, so much
so that I'm here as often as I am in Monaco and Paris . . .

It's a particularly demanding city, but at the same time it's a
wonderfully inspirational, dynamic, and cosmopolitan place, always in a constant state of flux. This book can only capture it
in the way a photograph can; who knows what it will be like in
two or maybe five years? But no matter how it changes, New York
will always be bursting with energy and creativity.

First of all, I would like to thank everybody who agreed to appear
in this book, whether restaurateurs, chefs, or artisans. I was
welcomed with great generosity and allowed to share their experi-
ences and emotions through their cuisine.

My thanks also go to Alex Vallis, naturally, for her help in finding all these places and for bringing a New Yorker's perspective
with the text.

Thank you to the designers and editors who took part in this
adventure.

— To Pierre Monetta, photographer, who understood the city and
  was able to capture its places and people vividly and up close.
— To Pierre Tachon, art director, who once again has turned
  my intentions for this book into reality.
— To Katie Mace, head coordinator, thanks to whom everything went
  smoothly, making for a serene experience.
— To Emmanuel Jirou-Najou, publishing director; Alice Gouget,
  managing editor; and to the entire publishing
  team.
— To Sonja Toulouse, Laetitia Teil, and Bénédicte de Bary.

And finally, thank you to my family for their unwavering support.

I hope you have as much pleasure browsing through this book as I
did making it and that you will feel the urge to discover my New
York, a city for gourmets.

                                                    Alain Ducasse

The editor warmly thanks Sonja
Toulouse, Bénédicte de Bary,
Aurore Charoy and Vianney Drouin
for the time and energy they
have dedicated to the making
of this book.

Abrams books are available at special
discounts when purchased in quantity
for premiums and promotions as well
as fundraising or educational use.
Special editions can also be created
to specification.
For details, contact
specialsales@abramsbooks.com
or the address below.

COLLECTION DIRECTOR
Emmanuel Jirou-Najou

EDITORIAL MANAGER
Alice Gouget

EDITORIAL MANAGER
Claire Dupuy

CO-AUTHOR
Alex Vallis

COORDINATION
Katie Mace

PHOTOGRAPHY
Pierre Monetta

ART DIRECTION / GRAPHIC DESIGN
Pierre Tachon / Soins graphiques
Thanks to Sophie Brice

MARKETING AND COMMUNICATION MANAGER
Camille Gonnet

PHOTO-ENGRAVING
Nord Compo

Printed in China
Legal deposit : 1st quarter 2013
ISBN : 978-1-61769-044-0

©Alain Ducasse Publishing 2012
84, avenue Victor Cresson
92 130 Issy-les-Moulineaux

www.alain-ducasse.com

ABRAMS
THE ART OF BOOKS SINCE 1949

115 West 18th Street
New York, NY 10011
www.abramsbooks.com

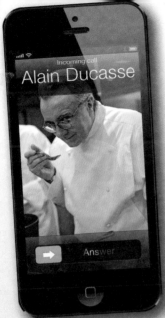

Locate and book a table at your local
Alain Ducasse restaurant with your iPhone

Cook with the iPad app: My Culinary Encyclopedia

250 recipes, 180 ingredient profiles, 100 video techniques

Download Alain Ducasse's books
on all of your tablets

Also available on **www.alain-ducasse.com**

ALAIN DUCASSE
PUBLISHING